"Payne's careful, detailed study of *90 Days of Believing God* should be able to put to rest any doubt about what it takes to initialize spiritual formation in the life of the believer. I strongly urge pastors and Christian education directors to read this book before they attempt to establish or revise the teaching ministries of their churches."

— **Lawrence C. Kirk**
Director of Christian Education
St. John Missionary Baptist Church
Oklahoma City

90 DAYS OF BELIEVING GOD

A Journey to Increasing
Your Personal Faith

RODNEY PAYNE

Twitter@PastorRPayne
Periscope@PastorRPayne
Instagram@PastorRodneyPayne
Facebook.com/PastorRodneyPayne

Published by Dust Jacket Press
90 Days of Believing God: A Journey to Increasing Your Personal Faith / Rodney Payne

ISBN: 978-1-947671-21-8

Dust Jacket Press
P.O. Box 721243
Oklahoma City, OK 73172
www.dustjacket.com

Dust Jacket logos are registered trademarks of Dust Jacket Press, Inc.

Cover & Interior Design: D.E. West / ZAQ Designs - Dust Jacket Creative Services

Printed in the United States of America

www.dustjacket.com

Dedication

This book is dedicated to my beautiful, loving wife, Thelma Payne. My life was forever changed the day I met you. I remember as if it were yesterday. You walked by, and I was overwhelmed by your beauty. As quickly as I noticed you, you were gone. Moments later you returned wearing a denim jean pencil skirt with a red blouse and a red scrunchie holding your long black ponytail. You had a box of popcorn in your hand, and I was at a loss for words. All I could think to say was "I like popcorn." You turned to share your popcorn as if to say, "Little boy, take some of this popcorn and get away from me."

As you know, the rest is history. Over twenty-seven years ago you blessed me by becoming my wife, and for that I am eternally grateful. To say you are my rock, the wind beneath my wings, or even the love of my life is to completely give understatements. You are my Proverbs 31 woman, and you are the catalyst for any success we have experienced on this wonderful journey. Thank you for loving me, praying for me, taking care of me, and raising our beautiful "little women." I love you with everything I am.

Finally, I would like to dedicate this book also to my mother-in-law, Rachel Richardson, and father, Kenneth E. Payne Jr.

Although you both have transitioned to heaven, I will never forget the unconditional love and support you both demonstrated. You both were so proud of us and gave sacrificially to make sure my family never went without anything. I miss you both dearly. Thank you.

Table of Contents

Foreword

I was raised in a "faith movement" and have been there all my life. I have many memories from childhood to the present day of being in church services where a faith message was *preached* with great anointing, authority, and power. I have also witnessed the simplistic, less demonstrative *teaching* style in which insights about faith were given with equal anointing, authority, and power. Likewise, I have been personally challenged, stirred, and encouraged by many writers who have shared their insights on faith--and many times I could sense that their *writings* had equal anointing, authority, and power.

While my life has been filled with many different forms of exposure to the subject of faith, trust, and believing God, like many other people, I have observed that often there is a disconnect between the proclamation of faith and the implementation of faith in the believer's life. This should not surprise us since 2 Timothy 3:7 declares that in the last days there will be people who will be "forever inquiring and getting information, but are never able to arrive at a recognition and knowledge of the Truth" (AMPC). Another insight suggests that there are people who never come to "experience the Truth."

While many have received countless amounts of information on faith, trust, commitment, and the importance of "believing God," a very limited amount of people have received the insight, instruction, and practical application that is found in this book. The result of a disconnection between what we believe and what we experience is often discouragement, disillusionment, and dissatisfaction, and in some cases it actually produces disbelief that is expressed through cynicism, doubt, unbelief, and even criticism of those who proclaim the truth and even the author of truth himself, God.

On multiple occasions I have had the responsibility of standing next to the parents of an infant child whose life had been either extremely short or marked by seemingly unbearable physical challenges. Whether the parents were Christians or not, the same questions about God and His plan, purpose, or tolerance of such experiences lingered long and hard in their hearts and minds. I've wept in my office with spouses who have been devastated by the discovery of an unfaithful spouse, all while doing their best to be faithful to God. I've sat in silence, not attempting to offer any type of trivial response to the individual who has been diagnosed with cancer or some other often terminal condition, hearing nothing more in my own heart and mind than the voice of the Spirit whispering, "Even in this will you trust me?"

Even beyond the crisis moments that might cause any person to question his or her faith and even God himself, I have similarly been visited by those who were experiencing an internal crisis moment as they searched for clarity and direction about their own personal relationship with God--and what salvation actually involves and what it really means to walk out their faith on a daily basis.

I believe I now have for the first time one of the most powerful resources available that I can share with those facing the crisis moments of all forms, while at the same time providing a stimulating experience for individuals simply wanting to take their faith to the next level. While this book provides a balanced theology on the subject of faith and believing God, more importantly it provides a strategic plan of action (an intentional spiritual journey or road map) from which every believer can benefit.

Whether you are a mature, established believer, such as a pastor, teacher, or leader, or a believer who has begun your spiritual journey but needs a practical road map on how to get from where you are spiritually to the next level of your spiritual faith and walk with God, this invitation and opportunity to experience the benefit of "90 Days of Believing God" is one you must not ignore or set aside.

If you are a fellow minister, read it, study it, and then preach it to your congregation! If you are fellow teacher, embrace it and use it as one of the most significant textbooks on faith available to us today. If you are a believer who is simply eager to grow in your relationship with God, open your heart and mind to experience real spiritual transformation. If you are a "pre-Christian" (as I like to identify those who have not yet come to know and believe on Jesus Christ as their personal Savior), I implore you to take the time to read and implement one of the most practical guides to believing God in our day.

As I have personally embarked on yet another journey of my own through this opportunity of "90 Days of Believing God," I have already been personally impacted by the experience. I can already anticipate that this journey will be one that I will regularly repeat knowing that each time the experience will allow me to go to a new level of understanding and relationship with God.

Terry L. Bates
Lead Pastor, Faith Church, Oklahoma City
Founder/President/Author of *Positioning Your Church*

Overview

90 Days of Believing God is intended to equip individuals to experience the power of God through their faith. This experience is rooted in a practical understanding of how to believe God. The reader will be taken on a three-trimester journey, gaining practical insight along the way to give foundation to his or her faith.

First, the reader will be taken through a series of chapters that discuss believing God from a personal perspective. The believer's personal relationship with God serves as the strength of his or her experience. Believing God must be a personal process.

Second, the reader will progress through the second trimester, discovering how to believe God purposefully. This trimester teaches the reader the "why" to believing God. Many times misplaced motivation can lead to a less-than-optimal faith experience. As the reader excavates the treasures of purpose, they will deeply enrich their Christian experience.

Third, the reader will receive direction to equip him or her to believe God from the correct position. Position identifies the point of origin for the believer's faith. Faith must always be initiated from the place of God's answer, not the place of the believer's requests. People who are to experience the power of God must access faith that tells their circumstances to relocate to the location declared by God. In other words, believers should believe from a place of healing, not a place of sickness; a place of victory, not a place of defeat; a place of liberty, not a place of bondage.

90 Days of Believing God is designed to equip the reader to experience the power of God every day in every area of life by increasing his or her faith. Enjoy the journey!

Rodney Payne

Acknowledgments

I must first acknowledge my Lord and Savior Jesus Christ for the calling He alone has placed upon my life. I am humbly grateful for God's choosing me to be a on His team. I am also thankful for the many people He has placed in my life who provide untiring support and encouragement in all He has called me to do.

I must first acknowledge all my family, friends, and the members of Bethlehem Star Baptist Church and my One Voice Ministries Team, as well as the entire One Voice family. The list of people is far too large to name everyone individually. However, I will name just a few people who never wavered in pushing me to complete this project.

I have a few mentors who have helped me grow in my development as a man, husband, pastor and author. Pastor W.B. Parker, Rev. Dr. James C. Coats, Rev. Lawrence Kirk, Dr. Sylvester Washington, Pastor Patrick Winfield II, and Pastor Gary Agee--thank you for pouring into me spiritually and pulling out of me the ministry God has placed in me.

Arthur and Barbara Campbell, from the very first moment of my pastorate you have supported my family and me with prayer, friendship, and support. Barbara Campbell, you pushed me when it seemed others had forgotten about the project. Thank you all for keeping me lifted up and holding me accountable to complete this work.

I would also like to acknowledge my friend, my road dog, my armor bearer, Keith Dixon. The many ways you support me, my family, and ministry are far too numerous to list. You are the epitome of a friend. Thank you for all you do. My ministry would not be what it is without you.

To my brother Thomas Brewer, your example paved the way and encouraged me to take this incredible journey of authorship! Thanks to you, Jenny and the girls, for your authentic friendship.

I would also like to acknowledge George and Denice Bland for sharing their miraculous journey of Believing God to add the overwhelming climax to this project. Your testimony gives tangible evidence to the power of God. Thank you!

To my proofreaders, my mother, Ephelders Lipscomb, and my daughter, Danielle Adams, thank you for your diligence in helping bring this project across the finished line.

Finally, words cannot even begin to express my gratitude for my family. Thelma, Danielle, and Devin--your unconditional love is what God uses to motivate me every day to become better. You have shared me with the world without ever complaining. Thank you for being the best blessing I have ever received from the Lord. I love you with all my heart! Thank you!

Introduction

One of the most perplexing dilemmas in today's church among Christians is that of gaining understanding in the area of faith. As believers we know that the very foundation of our existence and our relationship with God through Jesus Christ is faith. With the very essence of our existence being based on faith, it would seem that we would have a better understanding and a more universal approach to obtaining and possessing a personal faith.

Denominations have divided themselves at the point of who are the most preferred and greatest possessors of faith. Division has become such a point of contention that different belief systems have resorted to adolescent name-calling such as "Name it and claim it" or "Blab it and grab it" due to the insecurity associated with believing God, as ways of identifying the opposition.

If one possesses "super" faith, he or she may be viewed as a "holy roller" or even delusional. On the other hand, one who seemingly lacks faith has his or her salvation questioned. In this critical time for the Church, the body of Christ must find ways to unify and not divide.

Undoubtedly you have picked up this book for one of a few reasons. You could be looking to validate your faith process. You could possibly be looking to challenge the author's theology and thought process. Finally, you could be looking to transform your faith life as you have exhausted all other options for moving the many mountains of doubt, disappointment, struggle, sickness, disease, or financial ruin. Whatever the motivation, this book is offered as a practical approach to a well-rounded and complete faith in the power of Jesus Christ. The primary goals of this book are to transition the believer to the next level of faith, offer sound biblical teaching on the subject matter of faith, and learn to believe God from a personal perspective, a purposeful perspective, and a positional perspective. My prayer is that over the next 90 days your life your family, and your ministry will be transformed.

Three Critical Steps

The very foundation of salvation is a simple faith in God. In order to be eligible to partake of the benefits of believing God, an individual must enter into a personal relationship with Christ. John 1:12 states, "But as many as received him, to them gave he power to become the sons of God, even to them that believe on his name." This passage clearly puts the onus of believing on the individual, and the empowerment of the believer is to come from Jesus.

The first step to believing is to have faith in God. Hebrews 11:1 states, "Now faith is the substance of things hoped for, and the evidence of things not seen." This scripture has been used to define faith. I have heard many illustrations through the years designed to help one to understand this passage. Simply stated, one who operates in faith operates as if he or she has already received what he or she is praying for, even though the person does not have it yet. For the believer, faith must accept the reality and sovereignty of God.

Believers must never doubt the reality of God. Often people who profess Christ as their Savior will make the reality of God a contingency by statements such as "If there is a God . . ." or "There must be a God somewhere." These statements are not reflective of someone who is convinced and convicted that God is real. Let me assure you: God is indeed real. If ever you have trouble accepting the "realness" of God, just take a page from the "firmament book." Look around at the awesome display of creation that cannot be explained into existence from science. Just take some time to watch the beautifully clothed cardinal sing its morning song outside your window pane.

Faith not only embraces the reality of God, but faith also surrenders to the sovereignty of God. God is our self-existent Creator and answers to no one but himself. In the Book of Genesis the Lord clearly indicates that He will swear by himself, for there is none higher or greater. When a believer surrenders to the sovereignty of God, he or she is simply saying, "Yes, God--You are in full control." This is an essential part of our faith. Failure to surrender to the sovereignty of God can cause the immature believer to question God from an interrogative perspective as if to suggest that God has to answer to him or her. Remember: God's plans are far too complex for a mere mortal to fully grasp. So by surrendering to His sovereignty we understand that there are some things we will just not understand.

"By grace are ye saved through faith; and that not of your-selves: it is the gift of God: Not of works, lest any man should boast" (Ephesians 2:8-9). While faith accepts the reality of God, grace on the other hand makes salvation available. It is only by the grace of God that we are even afforded the oppor-tunity to enter into a personal relationship with Jesus Christ. Only when the individual's faith is added to God's grace can one be saved. Therefore, without faith an individual is unable to experience salvation. I realize that this is a very simple point; however, it is at this very simple point that many become con-fused. People spend far too much time attempting to be good. It seems this performance-based society has overvalued the im-portance of works. Many are not saved but spend a lot of time going to church and doing church work in an effort to be bet-ter "Christians." By no means am I suggesting that works are not necessary or that they play no part in the salvation experi-ence. Rather, I am suggesting that there is no amount of work that can get you saved. The work of salvation was completed on Calvary's cross by Jesus Christ himself. Because of Christ's work, believers have the opportunity to work. Therefore, sal-vation is not the result of work, but rather work is the result of salvation.

Second, believers must trust God. Proverbs 3:5 says, "Trust in the Lord with all thine heart; and lean not unto thine own understanding." In order for us to gain understanding of this passage, we must first establish a working definition for *trust*, and we must also differentiate between faith and trust. Earlier in the Introduction we established that faith believes in the reality of God. Simply believing in God is enough to establish a relationship with Christ; however, just as with any other relationship, a healthy relationship must grow. In order for us to experience true spiritual growth, in addition to foundational faith the believer must possess trust. For our working definition we will define *trust* as relying on and/or depending on God for everything totally and completely. In order to trust God, we must have complete confidence in God. A situational trust cannot be considered trust at all. When we trust God only in certain situations, we in essence suggest that the power of God is not necessary for direction in less critical situations. Another consideration is the eternality of trust. The eternality of trust is the single most significant differentiator between God and humanity. Humanity is only situational at best, whereas God is eternal. Trusting God is an eternal proposition with eternal benefits. While trusting on this side can yield some temporal results, the investment of "right-now" trust pays off best in eternal dividends. On this side of glory our trust will guide us through this tough maze we call life. Trust will help us to navigate through the perplexing challenges we face on a daily basis such as whom to marry, which job offer to take, or even what church we should attend. Trust also guides us through other life choices that may contradict our will. Trust will cause us to respond as did Jesus in His surrender to the Cross when He said, "Father, if thou be willing, remove this cup from me: nevertheless not my will, but thine, be done" (Luke 22:42).

Ultimately, trust does not save us but causes us to rely completely on God. Reliance on God is a simple confession of the inadequacy of the believer. Basically, we must be willing to admit that we possess no power to work through, overcome, or survive any situation without the divine leadership of Christ through the Holy Spirit. God must be the believer's source of supply. Believers cannot simply rely on their own abilities to supply their needs. As we begin to understand the ownership of God and the stewardship of humanity, we will then be able to offer the sacrificial praise God deserves. As trust leads to praise, praise can then be converted to worship--because God is worth it!

Finally, if we are to truly believe God, we as believers must commit ourselves. Dictionary.com defines *commit* as "to bind or obligate, as by pledge or assurance." Psalm 37:5 says, "Commit thy way unto the LORD; trust also in him; and he shall bring it to pass." It can be a very inexpensive proposition to say, "I believe in God," or "I trust God," as long as all you do is say it. However, the price increases exponentially when a believer actually commits to what he or she has claimed to believe.

Commitment is the process of putting action to your confession and proving out what you say you trust and believe. Many people put what is called a backup or a contingency plan in place for an impending failed first option. I am not suggesting that we should not think things through; however, I am suggesting that we should be willing to put all our professed faith and trust in the Lord and fully pursue His plans for us. The essence of commitment is not based on convenience or circumstance but rather on completely selling out in everything we do for a specific cause.

Many Christians believe they have received a specific vision or a dream from God, but they do nothing to actually make the dream become a reality. It is as if Christians believe God's giving the dream equates to automatically receiving the blessing. Undoubtedly God will show you a vision or a dream, but in order for you to possess or receive what God has for you, you must have faith in God, trust God, and finally commit to the processes of God. A genuine faith in God leads you to commit completely to Him. Commitment is a responsibility given to believers by God. Failing to take care of your responsibility cannot be credited to anything or anyone but you. It's up to you to hear from God by faith. It's up to you to trust the plan of God, and it's up to you to handle your responsibility of commitment to God. Too many times we as believers play the blame game. We are not walking in our destiny because of what someone has done or not done to us or for us. We blame our defeat on situational timing or just bad luck. As believers we must get to the point at which we are willing to receive our destiny out of God's hands and walk according to His divine plan.

Please understand: commitment does not save us. We are not saved because of the hard work we do at church every week. Arriving at the church early and being the last one to leave are not tickets to guarantee front-row seats in heaven. Simply stated, you can't do enough "good" work to work your way into salvation. Ephesians 2:9 says, "Salvation is not a reward for the good things we have done, so none of us can boast about it" (NLT) Commitment is a serving process rather than a source of salvation. Many Christians put more faith and trust in the effort of their work than in the grace of God. Commitment actually causes the believer to serve. When a believer is committed to the cause of Christ, you simply cannot stop him or her from working for the cause of Christ! Believing God is a process used to bless both the believer and other onlooking believers as well as non-believers.

God desires us to have faith, to trust Him, and commit to Him that others might come to know Him for themselves. The awesome thing about God is that He is willing to allow us to benefit from a personal belief in Him while He is doing His work of saving people and reconciling the world to himself. For example, a believer is believing God for healing. As a result of the believer's faith, he or she is willing to trust or totally rely on God for the healing. The believer's belief and trust in God then causes the believer to "commit his way unto the Lord." This conviction to commit causes the believer to spend more time in the Word of God. More time in the Word of God creates a more intimate relationship for the believer. This intimacy with God creates a cycle of faith, trust, and commitment. Before you know it, God has manifested healing in the life of the believer. Not only is the believer healed and thereby able to experience the healing power of God personally, but now he or she has a testimony to share with others for the glory of God.

You see, the three critical steps to believing God are a foundational requirement for the believer who wants to grow in his or her faith. *Faith, trust, and commitment* is more than a catch phrase--these three items are critical components for all who would experience the unfathomable power of God. As we move further through this process of believing God, it will be necessary for you to manage your mind by inspecting and/or altering your thought process. Philippians 2:5 says, "Let this mind be in you, which was also in Christ Jesus." Adopting society's thought process will derail your effort to believe God. The worldly influenced mind is unable to comprehend the things of God. God is ready to do God things in you and through you. You may have heard God-sized blessings described as supernatural, but remember: people define things as supernatural only because the natural mind can neither grasp nor comprehend the things of God. Therefore, just know that it is beyond your capacity to think through the process of believing God, but you must simply believe.

As we move through this book the goal will be to help you develop a consistent process of fellowshipping with God that leads to a fulfilling Christian walk filled with powerful manifestations of God's will in your life. Open up your heart and mind as we go through this 90-day journey of believing God.

You Shall Be Saved

Salvation--it's one of the more controversial subjects a believer will encounter throughout his or her Christian journey. The controversy between believers and non-believers is an easy one to grasp. Believers see the need for salvation while those who chose not to believe don't see the need for salvation. Although I don't agree with the latter, I do understand that because of God's love, mercy, and grace, we have all been given the opportunity to choose or reject the person of Jesus Christ.

The real controversy comes from believers. Based on denominational divisions, many have chosen to interpret the Word of God for themselves, thereby making their specific denominations exclusive clubs of Christians who they believe will be the only ones to inherit the kingdom of God.

My goal is not to debate baptism in the name of the Father, Son, and Holy Ghost versus baptism in the name of Jesus only, evidence of speaking in tongues versus confession, or one denomination versus another. Simply, my goal is to present a clear need for salvation and to offer Jesus Christ as the sole means of obtaining this great salvation.

Salvation by definition means to deliver from the power and penalty of sin. With sin as the predicament and salvation as the antidote, it becomes clear that salvation is a spiritual matter. Romans 3:23 says, "All have sinned, and come short of the glory of God." This passage of Scripture levels the playing field for all individuals. All is an inclusive word that does not leave anyone out. So while we may disagree on the process of salvation, we cannot successfully debate the need for salvation.

Regardless of your personal conviction on the process of being saved, one thing is for certain: you are not eligible to believe God for anything unless you are saved. Christians are often confused about how to access what God has reserved for the believer. You must know that not everyone is eligible to call upon the name of the Lord. Yes, you can call on the name of the Lord for salvation. However, those who are not saved do not have access to pray to God outside of a cry for salvation. In other words, as Romans 10:13 states, "Whosoever shall call upon the name of the Lord shall be saved." In this case, everyone is eligible to call upon the name of the Lord for salvation. The only prerequisite for salvation is the need to be saved.

However, once we are saved our relationship with God will cause us to call on Him for many things. These things are reserved for His children. The differentiator is the relationship. The problem faced by unbelievers is that they have not yet entered into a relationship with God but continue to call on Him to meet their individual needs outside of salvation. This is a great challenge, because many do not understand the relationship requirements. As a result, they have no perspective of the ineligibility of a nonbeliever. This causes many to charge God with not answering their prayers when in fact they were never eligible to pray in the first place. As we move through salvation, · we will be focusing on the confession, believing ,and security of salvation. If we are to meet our objectives in this 90-day experience, we must first establish our eligibility.

Romans 10:9 says, "If thou shalt confess with thy mouth the Lord Jesus, and shalt believe in thine heart that God hath raised him from the dead, thou shalt be saved." We have already established that salvation means to be delivered from the power and penalty of sin. The power of sin is to keep you out of the will of God. Sin's sole focus is to separate you from your holy God while on this earthy journey. The only weapon of the enemy is sin. It doesn't matter how it manifests itself--sin is the source of life's problems for the believer. Sin is transgressing the will of God. There is no way we can believe God while we are caught up in sin.

The first step in receiving salvation is to confess with one's mouth the Lord Jesus. Confession can be defined as an acknowledgement of God or entering into a covenant with God through Jesus Christ. With our eligibility being contingent upon salvation, a clear understanding of our confession is critical. First, let's deal with acknowledgement. In order for us to acknowledge God, we must first recognize His sovereignty. God already knows that He is self-existent. He is keenly aware of His omnipotence, omnipresence, and omniscience. The question is not whether God is God--the question is whether we acknowledge it. Are we willing to acknowledge Him as sovereign God with our lives?

Many people stumble when it comes to acknowledging the sovereignty of God. Most will readily acknowledge some higher power or a universal god, if you will, but the reality of God must be personally acknowledged in order for one to enter into this wonderful salvation relationship.

Once we understand and are willing to acknowledge the sovereignty of God, we must move from one who is willing to one who actually acknowledges. The key to acknowledging God is confessing Christ as the Son of God. Christianity is based on a salvation need that can be satisfied only by receiving the perfect sacrifice, Jesus Christ, God's only Son, as our Lord and Savior. This confession acknowledges God as God and Jesus as the manifestation of God's grace, as the one who saves.

Not only is confession acknowledgement of God, but confession is also agreement with God, which can be challenging for individuals. The fact of the matter is that we as believers would really prefer to agree with God only when agreement is convenient for us, fits our schedules, or doesn't take us too far out of our comfort zones. Agreement with God must cover every area of the believer's life.

Many believers are willing to believe God with their money or their health simply because everyone desires to be rich and healthy. However, when we go down the obedience and/or sacrifice track, we seem to drop off in our willingness to "believe" God. Everyone seems to be okay with God meeting their selfish demands wrapped in a token offering of doing a little good. The problem with this process is that such believers have put themselves first. They have established that a personal relationship with Christ is all about what Christ can do for them.

One of President John Fitzgerald Kennedy's most famous quotes was "Ask not what your country can do for you. Ask what you can do for your country." I believe this is a very profound quote that genuinely deals with the attitude of entitlement many Americans felt in the 1960s. Unfortunately, this great quote could also easily be adapted and applied to many in the twenty-first century, summarizing the approach many would-be believers take with God today. They are all in as long as the blessings are coming their way, but they are unwilling to pay any price or make any investment without a predetermined or pre-specified return. Confession is a position of agreement with the sum total of God, in every area and in every capacity. It goes well beyond what one can get from God.

Once we truly align our confession with God, we are much better equipped to accept His ways. We understand that God is in charge and that He alone has the authority and power to establish the rules we are to live by. Our confession is our agreement and acceptance of God's ways. Our confession is indicative of not only our acceptance of God's ways but also His power. God is not limited to being the one who makes the rules, but He also holds the distinct office of the only one who can make it happen. Your confession is your agreement that God will make all the rules in your life and that He will make His personalized plans for your life a reality.

Confession is critical as it is the agreement component of our salvation in Christ. Our confession must grow to a salvation that believes. Believing according to Romans 10:9 can be considered your personal conviction: "Because if you acknowledge and confess with your lips that Jesus is Lord and in your heart believe (adhere to, trust in, and rely on the truth) that God raised Him from the dead, you will be saved" (AMPC). Conviction takes us from just saying we believe something to actually doing something or moving on what we believe.

The first step a person must take in the believing process is to deal with his or her thoughts. Conviction accesses your spirit through your mind. In order to move on conviction, you must align your mind. Of course, that is easier said than done. How do you deal with something as fickle and unstable as your mind? First, you must understand that your mind should be responsive to your spirit. Many of us allow our minds to run away with us, and our thoughts end up taking us places we would never voluntarily go. The problem really worsens as we feel that we are losing control and have become subject to our minds. The key is to allow your true convictions to impact your thoughts. When you really believe something, you must discipline your mind to think on these things.

In cults the primary goal is to gain control of the mind through brainwashing. Brainwashing as defined by dictionary. com is "a method of systematically changing attitudes or altering beliefs." This definition provides real insight as it relates to the power of the mind. If you want to gain true control of anyone, you must first gain control of his or her mind. This process is often exposed when people leave the church in favor of "another" religion or belief system. They have been introduced to another way of "thinking" that has challenged their belief system, ultimately luring them away from the faith. If we are truly going to believe God, we must be convicted. As a result of our conviction, we must be firmly rooted and grounded in the Word. Our grounding will allow us to control and discipline our thoughts as we begin to act upon our convictions. Once we align our minds, actions will follow. The key to believing God in our salvation is acting on what we believe. A strong conviction creates action. For instance, if someone in your life who from your personal experience is known to be unreliable makes you a promise, generally you will not change your plans based on the person's promise, because you really don't believe he or she will follow through. On the other hand, if someone else with a much better track record makes you a similar promise, since you have a positive history with that person, you believe him or her and make your plans based on the promise the person has made to you.

Believing God is much the same process. Since God is unable to lie or fail and has an impeccable record of coming through for you, your actions should be reflective of His performance. If we truly believe God is our salvation, we must demonstrate our confidence in our actions.

Please understand that believing God is not an event but rather a continual process. It's not enough to be convicted in a crisis--we must live out our convictions every day and in every way. Understand that salvation is not simply an experience that ends at the altar--salvation must be worked out. Philippians 2:12 says it in this manner: "Wherefore, my beloved, as ye have always obeyed, not as in my presence only, but now much more in my absence, work out your own salvation with fear and trembling." The New Living Translation of the Bible states these words as "Work hard to show the results of your salvation." As such, salvation must produce results. These results require continuous believing. Life will present you with circumstances that will either produce opportunities to believe or opportunities that become roadblocks to believing in your salvation. The determining factor will be your willingness to be consistent in your convictions.

One of the more familiar passages in the Bible is 2 Corinthians 5:17: "If any man be in Christ, he is a new creature: old things are passed away; behold, all things are become new." Salvation in itself does not make everything in your life new at the moment of salvation. It is true that your spirit is renewed at the point of salvation, but you are still wrapped in the same sinful, contrary, decaying flesh. In salvation your flesh must still be dealt with. Just because you went through your salvation experience doesn't mean your mind suddenly ceases to consider sin.

Yes, everything is becoming new. Becoming means that a process must be involved. Too many times pastors, church leaders, or the outreach team have misrepresented this great salvation as an immediate eraser of the past sin stains left on your life. While that is true as it relates to your spirit, there still remains the consequences of your pre-salvation life to deal with. For instance, if you are $100,000 in debt and you get saved, your $100,000 debt is not immediately cancelled because you are saved. However, your salvation will teach you a new way to live to avoid such debt traps of the devil going forward. You must engage in an ongoing process of believing God. Yes, salvation is believing.

Finally, there is the security of salvation. Normally when you hear of security and salvation there is a tendency to jump to that old phrase "Once saved, always saved." Our focus here remains in Romans 10:9. The final portion of that verse states, "Thou shalt be saved." As we work through this concept, salvation offers eternal benefits not offered from any other source. As previously discussed in this chapter, there is much more to salvation than just a one-time event. Although salvation is initiated with an event, it goes much further than the initial decision for Christ. If a believer is to be saved, he or she will continue to grow in Christ. The growth is not for the purpose of maintaining salvation; rather, the growth occurs as a result of salvation.

In essence, salvation offers the believer security or protection from the results of sin. Sin at its core is designed to destroy the believer. It's really just that simple. The enemy is not concerned about his pre-determined fate of eternal damnation. He understands his fate and knows there is nothing he can do to change it. However, that will not stop the enemy from trying to get to you. One thing is certain, the enemy is coming for anyone who professes salvation in an effort to strip him or her of the benefits of salvation.

Salvation offers the believer protection from the enemy that will allow him or her to experience the benefits of Christ. The enemy knows he is unable to impact your salvation without your help. He is keenly aware of his powerless position when the hand of God is covering you. This is clearly referenced in the Book of Job.

Let's take a look at a brief portion of this encounter in Job 1:8-12:

Then the LORD asked Satan, "Have you noticed my servant Job? He is the finest man in all the earth. He is blameless--a man of complete integrity. He fears God and stays away from evil." Satan replied to the LORD, "Yes, but Job has good reason to fear God. You have always put a wall of protection around him and his home and his property. You have made him prosper in everything he does. Look how rich he is! But reach out and take away everything he has, and he will surely curse you to your face!" "All right, you may test him," the LORD said to Satan. "Do whatever you want with everything he possesses, but don't harm him physically." So Satan left the LORD's presence (NLT).

The first thing we notice is Satan's understanding of God's protection and favor. Satan refers to this protection as a wall or a hedge. Realizing he is unable to penetrate this wall, he is unwilling to even make a run at Job. The Lord asks Satan, "Have you noticed my servant Job?" The fortress God places around His children is impenetrable without His permission. As a result, we as believers are able to have the unshakeable peace of God through the protection of our salvation.

This wonderful protection acts as an initial peripheral protection. However, there are instances when God will choose to allow the enemy direct access to one of His faithful servants. Please understand: Job was not chosen because God wanted to punish him, but rather he was chosen that the glory of God might be manifested through him. You see, everything Job lost, every pain or sickness he endured, was for the benefit of the family of God.

As believers, we will certainly go through trying, difficult, or even tragic times, but the benefit of salvation is that we have undeniable access to the benefits of God. We have the exclusive opportunity to experience the power of God. I say exclusive because the blessing power of God is reserved for His children.

Not only does the security of salvation protect the believer from the results of sin, but it also seals the believer to Christ. Ephesians 4:30 defines the sealing of the believer this way: "Do not bring sorrow to God's Holy Spirit by the way you live. Remember, he has identified you as his own, guaranteeing that you will be saved on the day of redemption" (NLT). The King James Version uses the phrase "sealed unto the day of redemption." This takes security to another level. As we can clearly see by this text, the Holy Spirit is a part of this wonderful salvation, and He is the "sealing" agent. As the One who resides in us, the Holy Spirit becomes not only as our teacher and guide but also our guarantee. Salvation avails the believer to the reality of the Holy Spirit in his or her life. What wonderful assurance—to know you belong to God and are sealed by the Holy Spirit!

Let's be clear: we are talking about assurance and not a license. Many individuals have somehow concluded that salvation means a free right to sin. That thought couldn't be farther from the truth. Remember: your flesh is always at war with God, which is why believers never escape the temptations of sin. A true believer in Christ cannot knowingly sin without conviction by the Holy Spirit. Because the Holy Spirit lives in the believer, He will monitor when sin enters. The entrance of sin into the believer grieves the Holy Spirit, and in turn He will convict the believer for his or her own protection. He is always working to keep you clean and to keep you saved. There is great security in salvation.

That I May Know Him

Salvation in itself is the most life-changing experience any person will ever encounter. Just think about entering into an eternal relationship with the one and only true and living God. How unfathomable is the process of a wretched, unclean, hell-bound sinner coming to the eternal cleansing of Jesus Christ! While this is mindboggling, the believer can be even more challenged as it relates to understanding the person of Jesus Christ.

Just imagine: you are excited about entering a new relationship with a very special person. Now there are several things about the other person that you are attracted to for various reasons, but the truth of the matter is that there is more about the person that has not yet been revealed than what you already know. What a quandary! You like what you see and are willing to enter a relationship, but you really don't have any idea of what you are getting yourself in to. You experience both excitement and fear simultaneously. You are eager yet cautious.

While you are looking to learn about that person, you are deliberately withholding information regarding some of your less-endearing qualities. You seek to find out the truth about the person while presenting only the best you have to offer. You go through great pain to make sure you polish whatever blemishes the person may be able to uncover on his or her own about you while at the same time you enlist the help of your friends, the Internet, and any other resource that might help identify what's behind this person you are now attracted to.

We don't necessarily approach our new relationship with Jesus much differently. We approach Jesus as if we want to get to know Him on our terms. We erroneously assume that He doesn't know the real us, so we seek to keep that identity hidden. We must remember that we entered a relationship with Jesus only because we were sinners who needed a Savior.

So how do we grow from our place of deception and confusion to a place in which we actually come to know Jesus? How do we overcome the fear of the unknown while embracing this new relationship? We must come to know Jesus in a personal and intimate way. Yes, salvation is our introduction to Him, but we must go well beyond an introduction to build a relationship with Jesus that allows us to believe God.

Understanding the reality of a relationship with Jesus is difficult enough in itself, but to even consider coming to know Jesus Christ in a personal way seems nothing short of impossible for most believers. To do so, there must be a realization of His power for every believer. Not only must we come to realize

His power, but we must also be willing to participate in His sufferings. Last, we must identify with His death.

Philippians 3:10 (AMPC) says,

[For my determined purpose is] that I may know Him [that I may progressively become more deeply and intimately acquainted with Him, perceiving and recognizing and understanding the wonders of His Person more strongly and more clearly], and that I may in that same way come to know the power outflowing from His resurrection [which it exerts over believers], and that I may share His sufferings as to be continually transformed [in spirit into His likeness even] to His death, [in the hope].

In order for us believers to really begin to know Christ, we must realize the power of Jesus Christ.

The power of Christ is simply beyond man's comprehension. When we think of it, we generally limit the discussion to the providing power of God. It's almost as if we consider God a genie who grants each lucky believer three wishes. Interestingly enough, dictionary.com defines a genie as a spirit or a demon. How befitting! Believers take Jesus out of context and actually approach Him and expect Him to act as a genie or a demon. So the dilution or minimization of Jesus' power has been contaminated as well as limiting the believerss understanding of God's power.

The power that Christ possesses is unimaginable. Consider the power of Christ to overcome death through resurrection. Christ's connection to His Father afforded Him the limitless power of God as He suffered a crucifixion-sourced death. God allowed His only Son to die for the remission of our sins. God himself raised Jesus from the dead.

Can you imagine Paul's perspective as he considers the power of resurrection? In Philippians 3:10 he expresses a personal desire to "know" Christ in the power of His resurrection. Paul obviously believes in the power of Christ. He has personally experienced the converting power of God in his personal Damascus road experience. Just think--becoming physically blinded and staying in that condition for an extended time and then receiving sight again. This was a personal experience of the power of God that compelled Paul to want to know Christ not just personally but in the power of His resurrection.

The power of Christ can be realized only in faith. This realization is a turning point in the "believing God" process. As we become intentional in our pursuit of an intimate relationship with God, our faith becomes the cornerstone of our new reality. Once we know Christ in the power of His resurrection, we are positioned to live a life believing God.

As a prerequisite to knowing Christ in the power of His resurrection, we also participate in the sufferings of Christ. We all know that it is not human nature to seek to suffer. We spend our entire lives attempting to avoid suffering. Suffering according to dictionary.com is feeling great pain or distress. No one in his or her right mind would ever intentionally desire the discomfort of pain or the anxiety of distress.

I am not suggesting that we should desire sufferings. However, as a part of knowing Christ, we must understand that suffering is a part of the package. Now let's first differentiate personal suffering from suffering for the cause of Christ. Personal sufferings are self-induced pain or anxiety experienced as a direct result of our carnal decisions. Isn't it ironic that when we seek to satisfy our flesh, the end result is often suffering? How could the harmless end goal of satisfying my flesh end up in such a painful conclusion? The reality of our spirit man versus our carnal man is that there is no way to satisfy both.

Suffering for the cause of Christ on the other hand is suffering as the result of our relationship with Christ. Our relationship with Christ actually qualifies us for the honor of participating in Christ's sufferings. Remember: Christ's sufferings were purposed to redeem humanity. What an honor to be given the privilege of participating in the sovereign redemption process!

Simply put, if you don't know Christ personally, you are not invited to partake in this suffering. And suffering, much like praise, is not a spectator sport. To be in this holy bond with Christ, you will have to participate in His suffering. Your flesh will never willingly participate in suffering. In 1 Corinthians 15:31 (AMP) Paul states, "I assure you, believers, by the pride which I have in you in [your union with] Christ Jesus our Lord, I die daily [I face death and die to self]."

In this text Paul is focusing on the reality and relevance of the Resurrection. He indicates that a part of the process is dying to self every day. We must understand that our flesh has a way of resurrecting itself on a regular basis. It seems you have conquered a fleshly desire, and out of nowhere you find yourself right back in the middle of an old familiar sin. You sincerely believed with all your heart that God had delivered you from this sin, yet you find yourself starting down this road again. The key to overcoming this attack on your faith is to activate your faith. Activating your faith means that you control your flesh and you don't allow your flesh to control you. There is no way you can suffer with Christ and satisfy your flesh simultaneously.

So practically speaking, you must develop some behaviors that support building your spirit. As you build your spirit, you become better equipped to subdue your flesh. As a part of this necessary separation, you can become regular (not ritualistic) in your personal Bible reading and prayer. Too many times we get into regiments that we do because we are supposed to do them but don't necessarily gain the desired benefit. A personal relationship with Christ is one founded in faith, offered by grace and fueled by passion and desire. The passion and desire cause us to pursue an authentic relationship with Christ.

As a result, we understand the significance of suffering. While our human nature is not designed to allow us to embrace sufferings, our new nature leads us to embrace whatever our sovereign God permits to be a part of our personal relationship with Him.

Finally, now that we have a better grasp on the power of His resurrection and have thoroughly explored participating in the sufferings of Christ, we must also identify with His death. As previously mentioned, Paul lets us know that we must die to our flesh daily. This dying is symbolic to participating in the death of Jesus Christ.

As believers we must really identify with the death of Jesus Christ. Most believers are familiar with the public profession of faith through the act of water baptism. Baptism is a process of symbolizing how a person, as he or she enters the water, is born a sinner, while the water submersion represents identifying with the death of Jesus Christ. Once the individual is "raised" up from the water, he or she has "identified" with the death of Jesus Christ, having been raised, or resurrected, into a new life. Now I understand that not everyone subscribes to this specific practice in the salvation process. However, for the purposes of this illustration I am simply seeking to communicate a relatable process that helps us to identify with the believer's participation with the death of Christ.

The death of Christ was a horrific process. He was falsely accused, publicly shamed, and brutally beaten to pay for sins He never committed. He paid the price we were unable to pay. He did this because His love for us is so strong. Christ's love is, was, and remains strong enough to support the pain and agony of crucifixion for our benefit. We often quote John 3:16--"For God so loved the world, that he gave his only begotten Son, that whosoever believeth in him should not perish, but have everlasting life"–without even considering the price, power and purpose of His giving.

Christ had to consider how many times we would reject His love, how often we would abuse His love, and He also had to consider that many would be unwilling to respond to His great love. While wrapped in flesh faced with making the final decision, He had to take it personally and be unwavering in His obedience to the will of His Father. In consideration of Christ's sacrifice, we must do more than just be aware or cognizant of His death--we must identify with His death.

Identifying with His death literally means to partake of or participate with Christ in His death. Identifying is a personal process. No one else can identify for you. You cannot live vicariously through someone else's Christ experience. You must put yourself in the place where you can feel the stakes driving through the hands and feet of Jesus. You must feel the pressure of a crown being forced down on your head as the two-inch-long thorns pierce and penetrate your tender skin. You must feel as if you were down to your last ounce of energy while your side is being punctured by the Roman soldier's spear.

Can you imagine the pain Jesus endured? Keep in mind that Christ had the power to summon legions of angels to come to His rescue. He could have come down from the Cross but decided to subdue His own will in favor of surrendering to His Father's will. In order to identify with His death, we must make it personal. Habitually practicing sin becomes much more difficult when we consider the real price tag of such irresponsible practices. I know identifying with the death of Christ is not a pleasant process, but it is necessary.

However, there is another side to identifying. As we identify with the death of Christ, we must understand both the price paid as well as the reward granted. The death of Christ overcame sin once and for all. Yes, sin has a price of death, but the blood overcame the penalty. Ultimately Christ's death equates to victory for the believer.

Sin is the ultimate enemy of the believer. By nature, sin can appear extremely appealing. Sin is designed to kill the spirit of a person, but sin's primary weapon of attraction is targeted to the flesh. Sin disguises itself as a pleasurable process. Sin can be subtle in its approach while remaining deadly in its attack. Believers must understand not only the perceived power of sin but also the unavoidable destruction sin has already experienced.

Christ knew sin's capacity to entice our appetite for fleshly satisfaction, which is why Christ dealt with the ultimate power of sin once and for all on the Cross. Jesus has already paid the price to satisfy the death payment sin requires. However, too many times believers tend to dabble in sin just enough to stay in bondage to the enemy who has already been defeated.

If we are to believe God, we must accept His payment for our privilege that he paid through His love by giving His Son, Jesus Christ. Jesus finalized the payment by giving His life. We validate the payment through our willingness to surrender by receiving what God has already done for us.

Ultimately the death of Christ equates to victory for all who receive Him personally. As believers who are willing to believe God, we must believe that Christ dying on the Cross gives us victory over death, hell, and the grave. Our victory over death is manifested in eternal live. Our victory over hell is manifested in our reception into heaven. Finally, our victory over the grave is manifested in our participation in the resurrection of Christ!

So as you are on your personal journey of believing God, remember that you must know Him in the power of His resurrection. Jesus has prepaid your ticket to your destiny. According to John 10:10, you are the recipient of "life . . . more abundantly" now! Praise God for our opportunity to know Christ as we believe God.

Don't settle for being familiar or acquainted with God--get to know Him now!

For Christ Is The Head

One of the most important components of believing
God is order. First Corinthians 11:3 states, "I would
have you know, that the head of every man is Christ; and the
head of the woman is the man; and the head of Christ is God."
Order, according to dictionary.com, is "a state in which all
components or elements are arranged logically, comprehensi-
bly, or naturally."

In using this secular definition for *order*, we have to consider using a parallel approach for the spiritual and the natural. In
a natural sense the logical order would be the highest-ranking
official at the top of the pecking order moving downward to
the lowest. Additionally, the natural order would descend from
the strongest to the weakest.

If we use this natural logic in the spiritual realm, it would
look very much the same. According to 1 Corinthians 11:3,

Christ is identified as the head of every man, while God is identified as the head of Christ. As we endeavor to articulate the spiritual order required for believing God, we must become intimately aware of God's order for His kingdom.

Beyond the mere general awareness of Christ's superiority to humanity, we must willing accept the facts. In our acceptance of Christ as the head, by implication the believer is admitting a full measure of Christ-dependence. Christ-dependence is not situational nor is it a conditional application. If we are truly to believe God, we must understand that we must believe God in every area. In our recognition of Christ as the head, we must willingly accept God's order as the absolute governing principle for our lives.

The order of God manifests itself three ways in the everyday life of the believer. First, the order of God governs the family. Second, the order of God protects the family. And finally, the order of God redeems the family.

Many times the believer's faith experiences its greatest challenge in the area of family. As a rule, family members tend to let their hair down, so to speak, when they are home. In the home environment it is far too common to expect those closest to you to be the most understanding as it relates to your shortcomings. It's as if your family is supposed to understand that you have had a long day or that you don't feel like being bothered. Family members also seem to be more critical and less patient with other family member's failures. It just seems we as believers expect perfection from our family members while expecting them to overlook our degrading deficiencies.

On the other hand, we are more than willing to accommodate our peers, coworkers, fellow church members, or even perfect strangers for that matter. We will go out of the way for those we don't live with or don't know personally, yet we are willing to abuse our own family members.

Of course, this all changes when there is a family crisis. When we are in a crisis, we want to "pray together" to "stay together." We suddenly become willing to surrender to God's will for our season of suffering. As a result, many times we have inconsistent God experiences. When we apply God only to crises, we can never really know who God is or how He operates.

We must understand that God's order governs the family. The foundational principle of order is knowing that Christ is the head. Christ being the head of the family simply means He establishes the doctrine for the family. In other words, Christ gives us detailed instructions to both govern and direct the family. There are simple practices God puts in place as a standard for the family. In Galatians 5:22-23 the "fruit of the Spirit" is outlined: "The fruit of the Spirit is love, joy, peace, longsuffering, gentleness, goodness, faith, meekness, temperance: against such there is no law." In Galatians Paul is describing the "fruit" of believers. I find it very interesting that the Word of God uses the word "fruit" in its singular form while attaching plural characteristics. It would seem to me that all characteristics must be present in order to be considered "fruit." Furthermore, believers seem to be more willing to demonstrate the "fruit" with others but do not feel compelled to do so in the home environment. If there is anywhere believers should be fruit-producing it should be at home.

Not only does Christ establish doctrine for the family, but He is also the authority. When it comes to the guiding principles or doctrine for the family, we understand that the Word of God is the standard. However, I believe we assume and misuse the authority we believe belongs to us. Simply stated, God's sovereignty authorizes Him to be the supreme authority in His family. By God's position as Creator, He alone has all power and authority. This authority has been extended to the believer through Christ. In other words, we as believers don't have the right to "tell" God what to do. Contrarily, He possess the right to set the order for our homes, our families, and our lives in general.

With that in mind, we as believers must recognize that submission to God is a part of the salvation package. Willingly placing ourselves under the authority of God is how we become members of God's family. Although God is continually seeking to engage us in a personal relationship through Christ, He gives us the "free will" or the choice to accept Him or reject Him. It should go without saying that rejection of Christ's offer to salvation will at some point become the most regrettable decision a person will ever make. However, on the other side of the fence we find the single best decision one can make is to accept the salvation offered by Christ.

Submission is probably the single most difficult part of the salvation relationship. By comparison, if a person can get over the submission quotient of the salvation process, faith becomes a more palatable process for the believer. Submission is more easily digestible when you are the authority. In other words, if you are the person others are expected to submit themselves to, it becomes easier to deal with for you. You can readily identify with the fact that you are in charge. However, when the shoe is on the other foot, you become more interrogative in your process. When you are in charge, you clearly understand the chain of command and the hierarchy order; however, when your position in the chain requires you to submit, you require justification of orders, explanation on timing of orders, and a valid reason for the orders before you will even consider complying with them.

As believers, we know that the relationship is based on God being the supreme authority. So in our families submission must start at the head. The head of the family cannot expect the subordinate family members to submit when he himself is unwilling to submit. An unwillingness to submit suggests, we don't believe in the authority of God. If we sincerely believe in God, we are willing to comply with His order not because His order is restrictive but rather because we believe in the sovereignty and power of God. We know and believe that His plans are for our benefit. Therefore, as the head submits, this process is embraced by the entire family, thereby putting the family in place to experience God's power.

Not only does God's order govern the family, but it also protects the family. God establishes order in His Word. When we are willing to discipline ourselves to God's order, the family is protected. Understand that as you endeavor to believe God, the family will come under attack. Satan is not going to sit idly by while you believe God for your miracle and God changes your life.

The significance of the discipline in this process has been se-
verely underestimated. There are a few things the believer must
understand about discipline. First, when discipline is active it
derails Satan's attacks. Second, discipline is not automatic. And
last, discipline is worth it.

Discipline keeps us on the track God designed for us as we
stick with the script. Too many times believers like to call an
audible at the line of scrimmage. We know what the Word of
God says on a given topic, but sometimes we just don't see how
keeping this specific discipline will work in this situation. As
a result, we modify the plan in accordance with our thinking.
Of course, you know the outcome--we usually end up back at
square one or worse. Staying on the path ordained by God will
defeat any attacks the enemy may have planned to sabotage
our success.

Now discipline is a very powerful weapon, but it is not
automatic. We must procure discipline through a discipleship
process. In other words, discipline is gained from a discipleship
program. For the believer discipleship is an intensive study of
God's Word. This study usually has several contributing sourc-
es. First, you will have your personal study. This component
can be difficult for those who are newer in the faith, because
the Bible can be overwhelming as a textbook. Another source
would be a small-group Bible study. In this method you will
usually find a curriculum-directed study. This can be very beneficial since it allows the student to prepare prior to class, ask
questions, and interact with a group studying the same materi-
al. This is usually one of the more effective discipleship models.

One additional method you can consider is your regular weekly worship experience. Worship experiences are designed to inspire you to keep on fighting the good fight of faith. They should serve as a fueling station for the believer. However, inspiration without information will undoubtedly lead to a frustrated believer. Your journey becomes one of high hopes but often leads to disappointment sourced by misinformation.

As the realignment of order takes place, believers will become obedient through a personal relationship with Christ. A proper order structure will produce obedience, which aligns the believer with the perfect will of God. God has a very specific tailor-made purpose for your life. You can experience this purpose to the fullest only by demonstrating a willingness to live according to God's will for your life. However, this seemingly simple solution finds itself avoiding believers who are unwilling to submit to the will of the Lord.

Obedience is ultimately discipline in action. Desired disciplines can hardly be considered discipline at all. In fact, most things we would believe God for are nothing more than glorified wishes. We ask God, not believing that He will really deliver, so as a result we find ourselves having great plans, thoughts, or ideas but not accompanied by any action.

We as believers must grow to the point of following God's plan through obedience. When we follow God's plans, we ultimately protect our family. As we activate our faith through practice, we will see the consistency of God's manifestations in our lives. God is always consistent but can appear to be inconsistent based on our willingness to obey Him fully. Obedience signifies our complete and total dependence on the Lord in every area and every situation.

Through our disobedience we find our families lost and experiencing less-than-ideal situations on a daily basis. It has become overwhelmingly clear to me that families have become extremely proficient at faking it but never really making it. Because our families are so out of order, the desperation for a Christ intervention seems more like a myth than a real experience attainable through faith.

Clearly we must understand the sin attack that has overcome the family. Sin always leads us to our selfish carnal nature. As a result, believers unfortunately spend far too much time "separated" from God. Sin has a way of bringing about a very guilty feeling. When we as believers identify that we are caught up in sin, we should feel convicted, but we shouldn't feel guilty. Conviction is of God while guilt is a charge extended by the devil. So often our separation from God is self-initiated by surrendering to the enemy's charge of guilt. Please understand that we as believers could easily be convicted of our "guilt" if not for the justification of Christ.

You see, Jesus paid the price for our sin. When we have a personal relationship with Him, the Holy Spirit will convict us of our transgression to bring about repentance--while on the other hand the enemy uses guilt for the purpose of condemnation. The key here is to understand that Christ always overcomes the separation that sin causes. When we are willing to operate in God's order, God will always redeem the family.

Finally, the redemptive work of Christ on the Cross provides restoration for the family. If the enemy were to have his way, every family would be eternally destroyed. Families would wear generational curses as badges of condemnation. "But thanks be to God, who gives us the victory through our Lord Jesus Christ" (1 Corinthians 15:57, NKJV).

So in our effort to believe God, we must remember as believers that Jesus Christ is on our side! He has paid the price once and for all for our sins. He has made us to become the righteousness of God. Simply stated, because I believe in Jesus I have access to God the Father! No matter where I have been or what I have done, if I have Christ I am eligible for God's best! For Christ is the head of every redeemed person. Christ will always lead you to His Father and represent you as one of His children.

As you submit to the headship of Christ, your journey to believe God will become more fruitful and consistent. You are not blessed because you are worthy--you are blessed because Christ thought you were worth it.

It's Up To You

In Joshua 24:15 the Hebrew leader Joshua makes a firm declaration of a personal decision to serve the Lord. Although his declaration is nestled in a plea for Israel to make a personal decision for themselves, he mixes no bones when he offers the choice. He simply states, "Here are some facts you might want to consider, some things you might want to remember in weighing your decision," but he concludes verse 15 with a certain decision: "But as for me and my house, we *will* serve the Lord" (emphasis added).

If you are going to believe God, you are going to have to make a personal decision. The irony in making a personal decision is that many of our personal decisions lead us to a painful place of reflection on a previous "personal decision" that didn't go so well. How many times have you found yourself digesting a series of regrettable decisions that have led you down a seemingly unrecoverable path? You begin the painstaking process of coaching yourself up to make yet another personal commitment. "This time will be different," you tell yourself. "I have learned my lesson; I will not put myself in the position to fail again." You even decide that this time you are going to keep your personal decision to yourself. There is no need to bring anyone else into your personal business. You have made the determination that accountability partners are overrated and that all you need is the Lord to make it.

Unfortunately, you are not alone. Far too many believers experience this same déjà vu merry-go-round process in their personal journey of life. At the end of the day it actually is up to you to determine rather you will believe God or not. While we would like to say circumstances can drive you, people can also motivate you. In desperation you will find yourself forced into believing God--really, though, that's not the way it works.

You must be deliberate and intentional in your choice. Much like Joshua, you must take a deliberate inventory of your life and make an advised decision for your next move. In this chapter we will establish a three-step process of owning your decision to believe God. As one who seeks to believe God in every area of your life, you must honestly engage yourself every day to move according to your convictions. In making your commitment, you must take time to review the record, respond to the request, and finally renew your relationship with the Lord.

In Joshua 24 the leader of the Israelites, Joshua, is speaking from a historical perspective. You may have heard the phrase "History can be the best indicator of the future." I find this to be a very interesting statement, because there is biblical evidence to support this theory. The children of Israel are most known for their identity as repeat offenders. From one deliverance to the next disobedience they go, repeating the same bad choices over and over again. Maybe that's why we can so easily identify with the children of Israel--because we too find ourselves in the same messes over and over again.

Joshua uses this historical look as a challenge for the children of Israel to change their ways. He simply reiterates the many failures of their ancestors as motivation for them to make the right decision to truly serve the Lord.

As you review your record there are several questions that come to mind: How has God treated you? How has God treated your family? What has been your personal experience with God? Before you answer too quickly, there are a few more questions I would like you to consider: How have you treated God? How has your family treated God? Finally, how would God define His personal experience with you as one of His followers?

In consideration of the two-way relationship with the Lord, I am sure you were able to readily identify your shortcomings in the relationship. If you are completely honest, on the other hand, you will have to admit that even in the midst of your imperfect life, God has still been faithful.

Just as the Lord did for the children of Israel, He has repeatedly brought you out of bondage. Time and time again, you have received yet another chance to get it right, only to drop the ball again. Ultimately God has continued to bless you in spite of your sub-par performance. As one who is seeking to believe God, you cannot continue to respond to God's deliverance with disobedience. You must grow through your disobedient encounters. You cannot continue to willingly and joyfully accept the blessings of God while rejecting the responsibilities of the blessing.

The Lord indeed desires to bless us, and it brings Him great joy to do so. However, we are held accountable for how we handle this righteousness. Righteousness is received as a free transaction to the believer based on his or her willingness to receive what Christ has done for him or her. We must keep in mind that even though we receive righteousness at no cost, there was a great price paid for it. Our duty and responsibility to this great gift of righteousness is to handle it with great care as we honor every blessing the Lord shares with us.

So in your quest to believe God, make sure you take time to the review the record. Take a look back at how the Lord has dealt with you in spite of you. Take a moment to consider through all of your pain and disappointments, through your ups and downs, and even through your tragedies how God has still been good to you. On your journey of believing God, you must recognize that God has never failed you.

In Joshua 24:24 we see Joshua proceeding to force the children of Israel in to a decision corner. He doesn't offer an easy way out of a multiple-choice answer, nor does he give them the opportunity to write a short answer of misleading rhetoric to answer this question. He simply says, "Choose you this day whom you will serve." Yes he gives them some descriptors, but ultimately he tells them that the choice is theirs.

So I repeat the challenge to you as it relates to believing God. Choose you this day to believe God or not. You must respond to this request. This journey of believing God is not one you can take without complete commitment. You must be all in; otherwise what you are doing cannot be considered believing God.

Your response is completely personal. Many times as we embark on new life challenges and experiences, we like to get others to join us in the process. We can gain strength from the support of having others who are going through the same struggle. If I have someone by my side who can "feel my pain," it seems to make the journey easier to bear. The problem with a joint endeavor is consistent motive, purpose, and commitment. It is almost impossible to find others who are willing to match your commitment and energy levels. Either you are more gung-ho than your accountability partner, or maybe you just decided to join him or her for "support." Either way, you find yourself at different motivation levels, which makes it nearly impossible to support each other.

Spiritual matters can bring even more qualifiers to the process of accountability. You have to consider the faith element, spiritual maturity, or even the spiritual exposure one may have experienced. Believing God is such a personal process. If you have not been exposed to an active "God-sized" faith, you may restrict the capacity of God before you ever get started. For this reason you may have to realign yourself with people who have had greater experiences of faith. We know from Romans 10:17 that faith comes by hearing of the Word. So it should go without saying that you must increase your Word intake to increase your faith.

Having already discussed some options for increasing your discipleship process or "word intake," I will take this opportunity to focus on the contribution of leadership to your developmental process. Many times our faith presents itself as a regurgitation of someone else's faith. This is usually a leader in our life. Whether it is your boss, your spouse, or even your pastor, most believers are working from another's experience and/or exposure.

There are just a couple of quick nuggets I want to share with you regarding your leadership from a spiritual perspective. First, you need to understand how most of us operate from a spiritual perspective. Most of us are somehow compelled in a natural sense to seek God for a relationship. So it is the personal, "natural" relationships that really introduce us to Christ. That's why we see so many struggle when a special loved one passes away. The special loved one represents the individual's hope in God. This can leave us in places where we really can't choose for ourselves because our God decisions are not based on flesh relationships. So we actually do what we do because it is what we have always done.

Second, as we grow spiritually we begin to look to the Lord more for leadership and direction as opposed to convenience and gratification. When you begin to look to the Lord, He will direct you to the ones He has assigned to lead you in order to support healthy spiritual growth. So your growth becomes God directed thereby equipping you with the tools required to make better decisions. As a result, your discernment heightens and you are able to connect with leaders who can lead you to the next level. This next level of leadership is critical since your response to God has an eternal impact.

Let's take a look at how our choice to serve and believe God impacts our process. From the onset, when we delay in our obedience we also delay our blessing. There are certainly blessings in store for every believer, but our obedience is critical for these blessings to be released. Much as in our earthly relationships, we really can't make it a habit to reward negative behavior. When you have people under your leadership who consistently demonstrate disobedience, you don't necessarily want to withhold their blessings. You know that if you bless them in their disobedience, they will never find a reason to be obedient. This concept is really no different with God. He has requirements we must be willing to adhere to in order to receive what He has in store for us.

Our disobedience hinders beyond our own experience. Many times your descendants are impacted by your own disobedience. You don't hurt only yourself with your own disobedience. The transfer becomes generational. Just take a moment to make a personal inventory. How many challenges are you facing in life today due to previous generational decisions? There are many levels where we can easily identify the lingering effect of disobedience. One very simple example is the passing-on of a generational attitude. The command of Christ is that we love our neighbors as ourselves. We choose not to do so, and as a result negative disposition runs rampant in our families from generation to generation.

This generational process works for obedience as well. Blessed families seem to keep on producing blessed families. Ultimately your goal should be to respond in a way that pleases God, blesses your present, and leaves a legacy of blessings for the next generation.

Finally, if you are really looking to make the Christ decision, you really must look to renew your relationship with

Christ. In the Christian community renewal is often spoken of but may not be modeled. Your renewal process is more than just being sorry for "straying" away. Although renewal is the process of taking your relationship back to when it was new, there can be so many distractions and disappointments to clutter your thought process. There are just a couple of things you need to grasp in order to renew your relationship.

For starters, you have to release your past. The past has become such a powerful present condemnation tool. It's really not the external perspective that is so damaging. Yes, people will always try to convict you for your past bad choices, missteps, and mistakes, but the real damage comes in the court of personal condemnation.

Many times people are not willing to allow themselves to be free from the pain of past decisions and failures. They tend to build a personal criminal file against themselves, and under no circumstance are they willing to consider a personal pardon. For whatever reason, they just decide that they are not worthy of any forgiveness or pardon.

Let's take a little deeper look at the process of renewing as it relates to being free from your past. In the natural sense it can be very difficult to release yourself from something you can't forget (no matter how hard you try). One of the keys is to assess things from the proper perspective. You see, people tend to give themselves way too much credit for their success while judging way too harshly their failures.

One must really understand that it is God who gives the ability and grants the grace for any and all successes in the life of a believer. If we understand God's role in the success process, we can better identify with His role in the failure process. 1 John 1:9 clearly communicates God's role in forgiveness and the believer's role of confession. A better word for *confession* would be *agreement*. When we as believers agree with God, we are then positioned to experience Him in a new way. When I agree with God regarding the facts of sin, then I can better understand the facts of redemption. Sin separates because of my doing, while redemptions reclaims because of Christ's doings. That's right--my sin breaks the bond, but Christ's love restores the brokenness.

This process of redemption allows us to be renewed. This is how we progress to being able to release our past. The past is released not only by my Christ renewal but also by my willingness to receive what Christ has done!

Once you are able to release the past, then you can really begin the process of embracing the everlasting. You see, when God enters your life it is not a seasonal entrance. God's intentions are eternal. The beauty of the eternality of God is the fact of the immediacy of God's eternality. He activates your eternity at the point of salvation, thereby activing His promises in your life. However, it will take place only if you choose this day to serve Christ. Remember--it's up to you.

Share Christ!

As we transition to the second trimester of this book, "Believing God Purposefully," it is also time for us to transition to the next level of faith. This requires some measurement metrics to really have any chance of adding to our process. Keep in mind that you will never share anything or anyone you do not have a very definitive conviction about. Otherwise, what you are sharing could be considered only gossip at best.

In 2 Corinthians 13:5 Paul writes the following:

Examine and test and evaluate your own selves to see whether you are holding to your faith and showing the proper fruits of it. Test and prove yourselves [not Christ]. Do you not yourselves realize and know [thoroughly by an ever-increasing experience] that Jesus Christ is in you--unless you are [counterfeits] disapproved on trial and rejected? (AMPC).

You see, if we are ever to believe God, we must examine what we really believe. Growth can be measured in many tangible, performance-based ways for many things. However, faith seems to be proven only in measurable manifestations. In other words, we are not usually willing to express the faith we possessed until we have already been delivered from the storm. In order for faith to be considered faith, its activity must be present in the midst of the storm. Paul is saying to take a good look at what has been produced in your life as a result of your faith connection to Christ. He goes on to say not to test Christ but to test yourself, since Christ has already proven himself. Finally he concludes this verse by admonishing the Corinthian believer not to disqualify themselves or be found to be counterfeits. Ultimately it is up to us to measure our own faith through our own productivity in Christ.

In this chapter we will validate our "faith growth" as we look for reasons to *share Christ*. Let's further explore the motivation for sharing Christ as it relates to our journey of believing God. Christ has really given us a definitive motivation for sharing Him. First, Christ has perfect power. Second, Christ provides a productive plan. Last, He delivers us a perpetual plan. You see, Christ gives us a wonderful story to share, and in our sharing we are actually building our faith!

Let's take a deeper look at the perfection of the omnipotence of Christ. In Matthew 28:18 we find a distinctive differentiator between Christ and everyone else: "Jesus came and spake unto them, saying, All power is given unto me in heaven and in earth." In the Gospel of Matthew we find these words penned by Matthew as spoken by Jesus himself. He is very clear in His earthly form that He is the recipient of power sourced by His Father. At the risk of going too deeply into the various interpretations of the Godhead, let's just agree that there is power in Jesus Christ and that this power is directly connected to God. Let's also agree that any power of God is perfect and omnipotent. This perfected power rests in Christ Jesus. There are a couple of things we need to consider in order to fully appreciate the power of Christ.

Initially we need to wrap our minds around the power of Christ. You see, power exists in many shapes, forms, and manifestations. For instance, there is the manifestation of the power of influence. The effectiveness of influence is determined by its ability to influence others to move, conform, or buy in. We can conclude that the power of influence is contingent on another's willingness to adopt its strategy. While the power of influence most certainly has a place of effectiveness, it also has a place of ineffectiveness. We could also consider the power of position. People are required to respond in a certain way due to the position of someone, but that positional power in and of itself may not necessarily result in respect. Just because someone by position is over you and may even use his or her position to intimidate you into responding, the person's position cannot cause you to respect him or her.

Contrary to the supplied examples, the power of Christ is perfect and does not require your acknowledgment or agreement to be so. God in His infinite wisdom has granted His Son all power. You can agree with it or disagree with it. You can accept it or reject it. Your thoughts on the matter of the power of

Christ in no way affect the reality of Christ's power. Yes, Christ has perfect power, and that fact is non-negotiable.

With that being said, we must keep in mind that God gave Christ this all-inclusive power with an intentional love and purpose. This is where we as believers come into the picture. The perfect power of Christ allows those who would choose to receive this wonderful power of Christ as a salvific offering, to be eternally transformed. Choosing to accept the gift of salvation connects us to the perfect power of Christ. Christ is neither an unattainable entity nor is He an untouchable being. One of the most familiar scriptures in the entire Bible is John 3:16: "For God so loved the world, that he gave his only begotten Son, that whosoever believeth in him should not perish, but have everlasting life." God's love prompted Him to give His Son so believers could have both the source and the object of their faith. Jesus is the author and the finisher of our faith (Hebrews 12:2). Jesus is also the object or the goal of our faith. We believe God to please Him, and we get there through Jesus. Therefore the primary purpose of the perfect power of Christ is to give us access to Him and power through Him!

This perfect power did not come without a powerful process. There was a very painful process for both the Father and the Son to endure for us to have access to this perfect power. You see, power often appears easy to access, but we usually fail to consider the source of accessed power. Jesus had to vacate the splendor and glory of heaven and put on a dying and decaying flesh in order to give us direct access to the power of God. Jesus literally had to be born into humanity, be restricted as flesh is, and then, as if that weren't enough, He had to live a sinless life. Sin was the cause of Jesus' human birth into this world. If there were no sin there would be no price to pay, but because humanity had broken covenant with God, Jesus had to come to our rescue. Sure--there was the sacrifice process of providing animals as sin sacrifices, but God, in His desire and design to have a personal relationship with us individually, strategically planned a "once and for all" sacrifice of His only Son, Jesus Christ. This sacrifice was like no other. Jesus was perfect in presentation--He came sinless; He was perfect in living, as He lived without sin. Ultimately Jesus was even perfect in His dying as He endured the unwarranted shame and pain of the Cross.

What is the significance of all of this? The significance is directly related to how Christ received His perfect power. The process was very painful and could not be completed without a death experience. Jesus' power is perfected in His resurrection. The differentiator between Christianity and all other religions is Christ! Jesus received His perfected power in His resurrection. When God raised Jesus from the dead, He gave believers direct access to himself. So while we pray in Jesus' name, not only do we find that the ears of God are open to hear us, but we also discover that His heart is open to answer.

The perfect power of Christ is unquenchable. Even more amazing is the fact that God has given us authority to use this power. It is one thing to see power--it something totally different to have the authority to use this power. As believers we must be willing to share the true access and authority we have been granted though Christ. Even as we look back at Scripture, we can find Jesus' words in Matthew 28:18, as noted earlier,

"All power is given unto me in heaven and in earth." It becomes very clear that there is no power outside the power God has given to Christ. This is the power we as believers have been authorized to use. That is a story worth sharing!

Beyond the perfect power of Christ it is critical for believers to know that Christ also has a plan. Looking back at biblical history and processes, we see clearly that Jesus didn't call and save the disciples for no reason. Jesus called and saved the disciples in order that they might become team members whom He could give the responsibility of joining Him in His work to save His people from their sins. The real key to the plan is to know that Christ requires active participants. There is no way to believe God without active participation. In Matthew 4:19 Jesus clearly indicates the expected participation of the disciples: "And he saith unto them, Follow me, and I will make you fishers of men." In this same way you have been invited to join the Christ team as a participant in the process. It is unreasonable to think you can access God using the faith He has given you to get Him to give you the desires of your heart- -while not participating in sharing Him.

As one of Jesus' team members, you should see that Jesus not only requires participation in this productive plan but also requires obedient execution. Just the mere use of the term *obedience* is indicative of someone else being in charge. One of the most difficult parts of the process of sharing Christ, as we believe God, is to come to grips with the fact that we are not in charge. I realize that we use various terminology to describe our power in God, our position of favor, and/or our ability to speak things into existence. While I am not suggesting the previous expressions are untrue or invalid, I am saying that even with the many liberties God has afforded us as believers, He has in no way granted us the ability to be in charge of Him! We have to be willing to receive the orders and then execute them. In the amazingness of God, He allows us to experience Him as we follow the course He has charted for us. There is no better passage in the Bible to describe how God leads His followers than Psalm 37:23: "The steps of a [good] man are directed and established by the Lord when He delights in his way [and He busies Himself with his every step]" (AMPC). God directs our steps when we delight in His way, not ours. As we execute the orders of God, we, "modern-day disciples," must be willing to teach or share this process with others. God never has just one single person in mind as He directs. Just think about the experiences you have witnessed and seen others go through. Although they belonged to someone else, their experiences became your blessing. God will cause everything we go through to bless us while simultaneously blessing others. Obedience keeps us on track and helps us to avoid many of life's trials and tribulations. Sharing Christ through these experiences is a prerequisite for future deliverance.

As we are willing to embrace the productive plan of Christ, then we are ready to walk in to the perpetual promises of God. Doesn't that sound exciting? The perpetual promises of God mean that the promises of God that have no end date! Just imagine: once you begin to really believe God and experience His promises in your life, you will enter into a place in which the limitlessness of God's promises abide! This sounds too good to be true. I am sure that if I could convince you that this is true, you would have no problem sharing this kind of Christ, right? Well, I am telling you in no uncertain terms that the promises of God are delivered in perpetuity to believers!

Now before you convince yourself that this can't really be true, let me validate this line of thinking. Before you can really enter into the promises of God, you must understand that your qualification is not in your perfection, but rather your qualification is based on the unconditional love of God. The love God has for you is based on Him as your Creator. The love Christ has for you is based on God's placing you in His care. The Holy Spirit's love for you is based on His assignment to you from Christ. Ultimately, the unconditional love of God does not rest on you because you deserve it. God is not the source of love; rather, according to 1 John 4:8, "God *is* love" (emphasis added). The love of God reaching us in our sinful state is a miracle. But God goes even further than that. He goes from His love reaching us to His love making us eligible to receive His promises. 2 Corinthians 1:20 says, "All the promises of God in him are yea, and in him Amen, unto the glory of God by us." God says yes to His promises in your life because He has chosen to make you eligible! Consider trying to keep this news to yourself. The narrative would read something like this: "God has chosen me to be on His team. He sent Jesus to ensure that my eligibility wouldn't be in danger because of my sin. He goes even further to give me authority through the name of Jesus to access His promises." Wow--this story would be too good to keep to yourself. You would have to share Christ because of all He brings to you.

Before we conclude this chapter, we must consider one final component of this perfect power of Christ. While we have talked about our perpetual access, we still need to investigate the topic of how this power is supplied. In order for these perpetual promises to be afforded to us, the promises must have a limitless source of supply. Honestly, this is one of the most exciting topics for me to discuss. In short, God, the Self-Existent, Almighty and Eternal Supreme Being, is the source. Please be clear on this point. God is not a resource. God does not go and find power and then re-source that power to His children. No, God is not a resource. He is the source. God is the originator of power.

What does that mean to the believer? Simply stated, when you have a God need, there is no committee to determine your credit worthiness. Your worthiness has been pre-approved by God because you have proper covering. Your proper covering is the blood of Jesus Christ! You don't work your way into this covering--you receive the gift of salvation through Christ. When this part of the journey is accomplished, you will begin to experience the eternal power of God. You can have confidence the Lord will never fail you! No matter what the situation or the circumstance, you can rest assured that God will never fail you, and for that reason you can share Christ without any reservation.

When believing God we must have a pure purpose. Our purpose is not for our own greed or power--our purpose in believing God should always begin with sharing who Jesus Christ really is. When your purpose exceeds your request, your purpose will make up the difference between your faith and your deficiency. Share Christ--because He alone is your source, and He will provide.

Lift The Savior Up

Continuing on this believing God journey, the believer's purpose must be clear and properly aligned. Purpose misalignment of your end goal can decelerate the manifestation of the faith process. When your goal is ultimately for God to deliver you, bless you, heal you, or grant you increase, it is important to keep your focus on God and not the desire itself. Gaining clarity and understanding on the connection between process and answered prayer can be difficult. Let's take a deeper look into prioritization and direction of faith.

Believing God is a process that must be accessed in reverse order, or so it appears. It is natural to focus on your needs or desires, more than the process required to obtain your desires. To take it a step further, it is just as easy to forget the process required to obtain your desires once you have arrived at your desired destination or have received what you were believing

God for in the first place. You must take a deeper look at your purpose for believing God.

We must move from believing God for "stuff" to believing God because He is God. Our focus in this chapter is to learn how to believe God purposefully through lifting the Savior up. When our focus and priority list agree with the order of God, He will move us to the next level of our faith experience. There is much more to lifting the Savior up than wearing a cross around your neck or wearing religious apparel. Lifting the Savior up requires Christ to be exalted as Lord. As He is exalted, He will attract people to himself. Ultimately, lifting the Savior up unites the body of Christ.

Exalting Christ as Lord genuinely identifies the purpose of Christ. Christ would not and could not be our Savior without having the task of dying on the Cross to save us from our sin. Believing God requires a firm belief in Christ, and the believer must accept Christ as the access point to God. If Christ is to be the central character in salvation, then the Cross must also be considered central to the plot of the great narrative. The Cross serves as the intersection where sin meets holiness. The Cross serves as both an instrument of death and an instrument of life. The Cross was required because of our sin, not because of Jesus' shortcomings. Our sin is what separates us from the active power of God in our lives. So you see, sin hinders our process of believing God, but the Cross liberates us.

Christ was willing to die on the Cross to pay for our sin debt. Once we are willing to receive this great act of mercy and love, we must move from living on the grace of the Cross. We must understand that we too have a cross to bear. Your cross can be identified by the burden God has placed on you for His kingdom work. Your cross can be more easily identified through your spiritual gifts, which are special impartations by the Holy Spirit used to serve the body of Christ. In other words, as you operate in your spiritual gifts, you are in essence taking up your cross. This process could even be further defined as lifting the Savior up.

However, there is one part of the process we just can't glide by easily. As the Cross is equivalent to Jesus' instrument of death, so must be your cross. Death is only the first half of this great drama. After the death of Jesus comes the resurrection of Jesus. Jesus' death represents the end of living in the restrictions of flesh. As Jesus fulfilled the law in His living, He completed our deliverance in His dying. In our process of believing God we must also experience the death of our flesh. Paul states in 1 Corinthians 15:31, "I protest by your rejoicing which I have in Christ Jesus our Lord, I die daily." The real key is to understand that without dying there would be no resurrection.

Death signifies the end of one process, but resurrection signifies new life. If we are to believe God, we must exalt Christ as our Savior and identify with Him not only in His death but in His resurrection as well. If we are truly going to believe God, we must be willing to die to self. It is only when we die to self that we can genuinely begin to live in Christ.

As we exalt Christ, He attracts people to himself. Let's take a brief look back at the ministry of Christ. Jesus became famous for what He could do, as recorded in Matthew 4:24: "So his fame spread throughout all Syria, and they brought him all the sick, those afflicted with various diseases and pains, those oppressed by demons, those having seizures, and paralytics, and he healed them" (ESV). You can say Jesus really knew how to draw a crowd. This still applies today. When there is a move of God, people seem to show up from everywhere. The modern-day challenge is that people are looking for a miracle more than they are looking for Jesus. Don't fall for the miracle trap.

Now hold on. There is absolutely nothing wrong with miracles. On the contrary, believers ought to experience miracles as a part of their lives, but the miracle trap is when you ask God to perform a miracle but you have no intention of living for Him in that miracle. Miracles are not the reason for coming to Christ and serving Him. Miracles are by-products of an authentic relationship with Jesus. God performs miracles in your life through Jesus Christ for the purpose of attracting people to Him so that they might enter into a personal relationship with Him. Sure, you receive the miracle and the benefit thereof, but the purpose is to attract others to Christ.

Even when Jesus fed the 5,000 with two fish and five loaves, His primary goal was to attract more followers to himself. This story is outlined in Matthew 14:18-21:

"Bring them here," he said. Then he told the people to sit down on the grass. Jesus took the five loaves and two fish, looked up toward heaven, and blessed them. Then, breaking the loaves into pieces, he gave the bread to the disciples, who distributed it to the people. They all ate as much as they wanted, and afterward, the disciples picked up twelve baskets of leftovers. About 5,000 men were fed that day, in addition to all the women and children! (NLT).

The miracle of the feeding came after the lessons were taught. God has no intention of being a one-hit wonder in your life. His goal is to draw all people to himself. John 12:32 is probably the clearest presentation of this message: "And I, if I be lifted up from the earth, will draw all men unto me." Jesus must be the central character in our lives. When that happens, He will bless us with what we are believing Him for because we are in His will. His will is to attract people to himself.

Even beyond the crucifixion and resurrection of Jesus, He continued to draw men to himself. "Those who believed what Peter said were baptized and added to the church that day--about 3,000 in all" (Acts 2:41, NLT). Peter taught the message of Jesus, and then the crowd was compelled to ask the Apostles, "What shall we do?" Peter said to repent and be baptized. Basically the message was to attract people to Jesus and for the crowd to respond by entering into an active relationship with Him. If you are willing to lift the Savior up, you will not only witness His work but also experience His power!

So the question that every believer must answer is "What am I really doing to lift the Savior up?" As believers we should thoroughly investigate our lives to see if they're focused on lifting the Savior up--or are we more concerned with what we can gain from God? The real key here is to give God first place in your life and always consider your relationship with Christ as the most important part of the process. When your conversation is all about what you have or what you have accomplished, you have made this journey all about yourself. God's desire is to be the main attraction--not for what He can do for you but rather for who He is to you. As we lift Him up, He will bless us and give us increase accordingly. I cannot state this strongly enough. We must seek God and not His "stuff." The "stuff" comes through the relationship, but the relationship will not come through the "stuff."

Finally, when we exalt Christ, He will use us to attract people to himself. The purpose of Christ is to save people and unite His body. The irony in this whole process is that we as believers use the power of Christ to divide ourselves as opposed to coming together. Somehow we have wiggled our way into the mind-set that some of us are better than others. Somehow I am more saved than you are, and as a result, I have more "power" than you. This thing of "blessing competition" has caused a major power erosion in the Church. Instead of truly operating in the power of God, we compare our experience to other believers while all the time minimizing the power and effectiveness of Christ.

In the ministry of Paul, Christ is revealed as One who is available to all, Both the Jew and the Greek. Jesus did not die on the Cross to separate us. Jesus died that "whosover shall call upon the name of the Lord shall be saved" (Romans 10:13). We can see by the aforementioned scripture that Jesus is interested in saving all, not just a select few. Jesus never intended to play the background in our petty competitions. The favor of God is reserved for the children of God, and He alone measures out His favor. In our journey to believe God, we must take a wise approach remembering that it's really not about us anyway. We cannot allow the confusion of competition to disconnect us from the compassion of Christ.

In Jesus' dying for whoever was willing to receive Him, He removed the childish separations we are presently experiencing through denominational religion. We as believers all depend on the same God to save, heal, and deliver. Without Christ our life has no real meaning or purpose. Lifting the Savior up ensures that we have the right focus. Remember: God gives preference to those who are blood covered. In other words, your salvation gives you access to the preference of God. This is such a crucial and difficult principle for believers to grasp. God prefers those who wear His name. This preference is not over one another. This preference is in Christ.

Ultimately God's desire is to connect Christians, not divide us. When we were lost in our sin, there was a commonality that separated us from Christ. The commonality was found it the fact we were all lost sinners with no hope. But the cross of Jesus Christ brings us together as a redeemed people. Now our commonality is in Christ. We have been transformed from sinners to those who are now saved by grace. We all have eternal access because of the Cross. In our new commonality we have no need to fight over salvation, position, or preference because we are all in the same boat. If we didn't have Christ we wouldn't stand a chance. But because of Christ we can now be united.

As believers we must realize that the cross of Christ connects us. We must receive all aspects of the Cross in order to experience the power of God. When we receive the power of the Cross, we truly position ourselves to believe God in a new way. Give God the number-one slot in your life as you are believing Him, and watch Him respond to your faith in ways you may have never experienced. Once you realize that Jesus is the star of the show and you are willing to lift Him up, you are well on your way to believing God purposefully!

———————— ● ————————

Bless The Body Of Christ

As we continue our journey of learning to believe God, I have found that too many times we can get so caught up in the blessing we are seeking that we easily overlook the blessing we are carrying. God has personally placed in each of His children spiritual gifts. Spiritual gifts are God given and God purposed, however, and when they are not handled with care they can lead to strife and division within the body of Christ. Many miss the mark by conducting an inventory of other believers' gifts while simultaneously completing their own ranking system. The goal is to determine who is the most important or the most "gifted" believer, which can present a real problem with one's spiritual esteem.

When a believer begins to slide down the slippery slope of gift inspection, it can lead to an improper reduction of one's self and cause him or her to lose focus. It's like falling into a trap of asking God for misguided blessings that aren't really blessings at all. As we move through this chapter, our goal will be to look at God's process of spiritual gifting. We will uncover some facts regarding spiritual gifts. In this process of believing God we must learn that every spiritual gift produces evidence of the Godhead, every believer possesses at least one spiritual gift, and every spiritual gift is equally beneficial to the body of Christ.

When attempting to prove a case, a conviction requires evidence or proof of the allegations. It's not enough to merely suggest that something is true or untrue. In order to have any credibility, you must provide evidence to support the event in question. Generally when we think of evidence or a case, we think of criminal charges being brought followed by a jury and a judge determining the innocence or guilt of a defendant. In the body of Christ it seems we have become more interested in discrediting one's actions than believing God for the best in a given situation.

Let's direct our focus and attention to how spiritual gifts serve as evidence in the case for Christ. First Corinthians 12:4-7 states, "There are different kinds of spiritual gifts, but the same Spirit is the source of them all. There are different kinds of service, but we serve the same Lord. God works in different ways, but it is the same God who does the work in all of us. A spiritual gift is given to each of us so we can help each other" (NLT). This scripture provides us clear evidence of the variety, source, and purpose of spiritual gifts. We can clearly see that not all gifts are the same. In this journey of believing

God, Christians have seemingly become content with mimicking someone else's apparent gifts rather than seeking God for revelation of their own gifts.

The previously mentioned scripture goes on to further identify the Holy Spirit as the source of all spiritual gifts. It is critical for us to understand that spiritual gifts are not manufactured by a believer's desire. They are delivered in a customized fashion by the Holy Spirit. As you are seeking God, you must be willing to accept how He has chosen to equip you in your service to the Lord. In 1 Corinthians 12:6 Paul makes our individuality very clear while giving us a glimpse of the power of God. Paul is clear that we all operate differently yet God remains the same as He is working in us all. Personally, I find 1 Corinthians 12:7 to be one of the most profound scriptures in the Bible. In this passage Paul clearly states the purpose of spiritual gifts. As we continue our pursuit of believing God purposefully, we must come into agreement with the Word of God. Paul informs us with certainty and clarity that we are granted gifts to help each other or bless the body of Christ.

Now that we better understand the "why" of spiritual gifts, let's move on to the "how" of spiritual gifts. Every gift gives evidence of the power of God. The Holy Spirit operates within each of us, using spiritual gifts to give evidence to support the power of God. When spiritual gifts are at work, there is a visible demonstration of God's power. These demonstrations serve as evidence to others. When God uses spiritual gifts in us, it is for others' needs to be met as they witness the power of God in action. God is so wise! He knows we desire to see Him in action; thus, He gives us an opportunity to tangibly experience His power. If we are able to pull together a few resources and make something happen, we would be less likely to credit God for the event. When God moves, He leaves no doubt of His work.

God signs His "Picasso of blessings" by using mere human hands to perform the supernatural task. Godly manifestations exceed human ability. Human ability is limited in every way. First is the restriction of space. A person can occupy only one space at a time. Then there is the issue of power. An individual is limited to whatever physical strength and ability he or she possesses. This can be challenging when you are facing simultaneous, overpowering problems that are present in multiple locations. When God resides in you by the power of the Holy Spirit, He can activate your spiritual gifts on the inside and literally move you from the natural to the supernatural in an instant. You see, while *natural* represents your limited physical abilities, *supernatural* really doesn't refer to God. *Supernatural* is a term used by people when they don't have evidence to support the cause or effect of events. *Supernatural* becomes humanity's way of explaining the normal of God. The normal of God is beyond humanity's comprehension. The supernatural of God is best evidenced in His willingness to equip believers with spiritual gifts to work and produce mighty fruit to benefit the kingdom of God.

As we look to better understand how God uses spiritual gifts to bless the body of Christ, the question often comes up "Does every believer have a spiritual gift?" The answer is a definitive yes! This fact is made very clear to us in 1 Peter 4:10: "As each of you has received a gift (a particular spiritual talent, a gracious divine endowment), employ it for one another as [befits] good trustees of God's many-sided grace [faithful stewards of the extremely diverse powers and gifts granted to Christians by unmerited favor]" (AMPC). Peter lets us know that "each of you has received." He is referring to the spiritual gift from God for His service. It has become apparent to me that we as believers often have difficulty identifying our areas of gifting. There are usually a couple of drivers behind the gift identification problem. First of all, we are simply unwilling to seek God for the answer to the question. Somehow, since we are unable to identify our spiritual gifts, we feel as if we are exempt from the responsibility that comes with the gift. Rest assured--God has given us the responsibility to seek Him for the specific assignment He has given us. No, ignorance is not bliss! Beyond our unwillingness to ask God what He would have us do, many believers are "gift-seekers." A gift-seeker is one who is unwilling to ask God to reveal His choice in how He chooses to bless the believer. A gift-seeker is more likely to seek God for gifts based solely on his or her personal desires. This could almost be considered covetousness. One can desire so strongly to be used by God in a specific area or in the same manner as someone else that the person never really operates in his or her God-ordained spiritual gifts.

God in His infinite wisdom equips His children according to the assignments He has for them. As a result, your gift is purpose-aligned and purpose-assigned. God supplies you with what you will need to function in the capacity that He has predestined you to function. This can be very challenging for many believers. If you are willing to truly seek God for His will in your life, you will find that His purpose for you always exceeds your ability to see yourself operating at such capacity. Simply stated, God will blow your mind with His plans for you. Remember--God has gifted every believer with a spiritual gift to purposefully serve as a blessing to the body of Christ. For this reason we are not permitted to choose our own spiritual gifts; yet we are permitted to seek God for revelation of the spiritual gifts He alone has granted and to use these gifts to bless the body of Christ.

As believers who are seeking to believe God, we must trust the process. Your faith will always be effective in your destiny. When you attempt to believe in disobedience, you set yourself up for failure and disappointment. What's worse than failure or disappointment? Misrepresentation of God in the process supersedes both failure and disappointment. Too many times we blame God for our intentional misalignment. He has established a process for proper placement and an infallible system of equipping His children. Spiritual gifts are God's way of meeting His children's needs here on earth. Thus, you should make it your business to invest in your Christ relationship in order to gain clear insight and understanding of your purpose and your spiritual gifts. You are not waiting on God to reveal your spiritual gifts; rather, God is waiting on you to seek Him for what He has already placed in you. At the point of your conversion, you were already equipped to perform in your kingdom role. God had plans for you before you ever stepped foot on the planet. Let's walk in our spiritual gifts to bless the body of Christ.

Here is one final consideration as we conclude this matter of blessing the body of Christ: the significance of spiritual gifts. Humanity by its flesh nature has created some hierarchal rating system of determining one's value or significance in the Body of Christ. Every spiritual gift has a place of significance in the kingdom of God. I know it is easy to get caught up in equating the visibility of one's spiritual gift with the significance of his or her spiritual gift. However, that process simply has no merit. For instance, someone who is spiritually gifted in the area of administration may never be seen on stage, but the results of his or her efforts are always prominently visible. Administrators keep the ship on course, all the players in place, and the finances stable. Until things are mismanaged, they basically go unnoticed. When the system runs smoothly no one notices how smoothly things are going. This results in an unrecognized spiritual gift. Conversely, when things are not going well people begin to ask questions like "Who is running this place?" or "What are they doing back there with the money?" You see, just because a spiritual gift is not visible does not mean it is insignificant.

Please keep in mind that spiritual gifts are given for the whole body. This means that they are sanctioned to operate beyond your local church. Now please don't take the previous sentence to mean that you are free to operate recklessly with your spiritual gifts. Our focus here is engaging them in your area of assignment first and then, keeping in line with the Holy Spirit's guidance, extending your spiritual gifts to others. Honestly, the bigger challenge is remaining humble with your spiritual gifts. Remember: your spiritual gifts are assigned and empowered by God. As a result, there is no room for arrogance. Arrogance by definition is a first cousin to pride. In order to perform, you possess a high opinion of yourself and rely only on the resources you personally possess.

Spiritual gifts operate in God confidence, not arrogance. Your spiritual gifts are reliant upon the power of the Holy Spirit to perform. As a result, there is no room for arrogance or selective spiritual gift usage. You don't get to decide that you are too good, too qualified, or too gifted to serve in a given area. When you decide that something is beneath you, you are headed straight for self-destruction. As a believer, you simply do not have the authority to measure out your spiritual gifts as you deem appropriate. Your spiritual gifts are on a spiritual assignment. God himself is in charge of the placement! Don't get yourself into trouble by thinking that you are more important than you really are. It is impossible to believe God when you mishandle the responsibility of service God has given you.

Remember: spiritual gifts are God-given for His body. With that said, don't allow yourself to get bogged down in the minutia of performing to impress people. People have no part in determining your value. Your value is not assessed by people but rather assigned by God. We often get distracted by how others place value upon us. We must make it our business to focus on what God says about us. When we are willing to accept God's truth about us, it becomes much easier to bless the body of Christ. The process becomes much more purposeful and rewarding when we understand the God motive and the God approval.

Blessing the body of Christ ultimately enhances your Christian experience. As you believe God and bless the body of Christ on purpose, you begin to see firsthand how God blesses you when you bless the body of Christ. As you are willing to bless the body of Christ, you actually equip the body of Christ to be a blessing to others. When your attention goes to becoming the hands of God, your spirit is now in a place to receive His blessings.

God has a plan to respond to you as you are believing Him. His personal plan for you includes blessing you immensely. God has authored your faith to give you access. He has authored your faith to receive spiritual gifts. He has purposed you to bless His body. On your journey to believe God purposefully, you must stay the blessing course. The plan is far greater than you, but the plan does include you. Surrender your gifts today, and expect the best from God as you believe Him through blessing the body of Christ!

Build The Kingdom

The kingdom of God can be a challenging subject to grasp. In the modern-day church "the kingdom of God" is often shortened to "the kingdom." This phrase is often attached to other common phrases such as "kingdom-minded" or "kingdom-focused." The inference of the phrases is that the kingdom should ultimately serve as motivation for any believer's actions in "kingdom work." As we continue to thoroughly look at the process of believing God, we must seek to better understand how building the kingdom of God should serve as motivation for our beliefs.

We must first consider a working definition for "the kingdom of God." There is much research on this topic, but for our purposes here I would like to simplify the thought with the ultimate goal of expanding our faith process. As we look at kingdom-building, let's consider God as our King. As believer we live in His domain, and He alone has dominion. Let's see if we can reduce this one step further. As the King, God has all authority and power to establish the order or rules in His kingdom. Please know there is an appropriate way for things to operate in the kingdom of God.

Now in consideration of building the kingdom, we are simply suggesting that all our efforts in living a life of believing God should promote or build the kingdom. In Matthew 16:19 we find these words: "I will give you the keys of the Kingdom of Heaven. Whatever you forbid on earth will be forbidden in heaven, and whatever you permit on earth will be permitted in heaven" (NLT). This scripture follows the revelation to Peter of Jesus being the Son of God. As a part of His reply, Jesus tells Peter and the other disciples that He will "give [them] the keys to the Kingdom." This statement could really be viewed as Christ granting the disciples access to kingdom living. Jesus gives this access of bringing to life proper kingdom living on the earth. In other words, when Jesus grants the disciples "permitting" authority, He in essence is saying, "Wherever you are, you can experience kingdom living".

Building the kingdom is literally expanding your life experience to include a kingdom experience in every area of your life. Building the kingdom is to expand the number of people who have the faith to live this way. In this chapter we will look at a few practical ways to expand or build the kingdom on our believing-God journey. First, we need to establish the fact that the kingdom of God is not readily identifiable to everyone--it must be revealed. Second, the kingdom of God has nothing to be compared to, as it is the standard. Last, we will look at what is produced through the kingdom.

Jesus often taught of the kingdom of God or the kingdom of heaven using parables. The introduction quote often used by Jesus was "The kingdom of heaven is like unto . . ." This is Jesus' way of opening an example to give us insight that we could better understand in order to get a clear picture of what the kingdom of God is really like. Please understand that there is no way to identify with the kingdom of God if you do not have a personal relationship with Christ. It will remain a mystery to anyone who does not believe in God. The clock of understanding the kingdom of God starts at the point of salvation. There is no way for a person who is not a believer to understand the kingdom of God. The requirements of Christ in kingdom living will just not make sense to a non-believer.

There are principles a non-believer will not be able to grasp until revelation comes as a part of his or her salvation experience. Not to suggest that Christianity is a secret club, but we need to understand that there are only assumptions when looking from the outside it. When you are not a part of an organization, you really have only personal observation and hearsay to establish your opinion. There are no secret handshakes to get you into the "secret" kingdom club, but there is the price of salvation to gain access. Otherwise, everything in the kingdom remains a great mystery. This makes it very difficult to attempt to have a spiritual conversation with a non-believer, because there is just no common denominator on which to base your communication.

Once you gain kingdom access through salvation, the revelation process can begin. Revelation in its most simple form is to uncover or reveal. Kingdom revelation really begins through discipleship. In the believing-God process discipleship is necessary. Discipleship is the process of learning specific disciplines from a teacher. The uniqueness of your Christ experience is the introduction of the Holy Spirit into your learning process. As believers, we know that the Holy Spirit lives in us as both our helper and our power. The Holy Spirit helps us understand in a clear manner the things of God, or better stated, the kingdom of God. Think of the Holy Spirit as a translator. He literally takes instructions from God and translates them so believers can understand what God is saying. Once the translation happens, then activation can happen. The Holy Spirit activates kingdom principles in your life.

A simple faith is required to start the process, but there must be an increasing faith for increased experiences. Basically the more you know, the more you can believe, the more you can believe, the more you can experience. This is why there is more to believing God than just believing God. I know that the Church has made it sound really simple: "Just have faith, and everything will be all right." If only it were that easy. Faith requires attention and development. If you are unwilling to develop your faith, you will never fully experience God. Romans 10:17 states, "Faith cometh by hearing, and hearing by the word of God." You see, faith will never increase when we are not willing to "hear" or read the Word of God. Reading the Word of God serves as fertilizer for our personal soul growth. When we take time to invest in reading the Word of God for understanding, it will always pay a dividend of growth. The growth experienced increases our capacity for building the kingdom. As our capacity increases, God uses our faith as the foundation for our new revelation. God shows us to grow us. The revelation of God is directly tied to your spiritual growth and both your kingdom living and kingdom building.

Consuming more of the Word of God does not always grow us by revealing external things. Certainly God allows us to witness or experience growth through the life lessons of others, but He also has an internal growth plan. This plan works just a little bit differently. While things we witness are good, things we experience can be even better. God will grow us through our trials and increase our kingdom-building capacity. In other words, as you go through life's challenges, you gain firsthand knowledge of how God operates (kingdom principles) in real-life situations. God uses everything about the situation to reveal more of himself to you.

Just think about it: often when we are going through the fire of trials, we are not learning but rather living through the process. However, at some point beyond the crisis we find ourselves being able to look back and learn the lesson that was in the trial. This is the revelation of God! Now the trial is transformed into a testimony. You survived the test, and now you can testify better than an eyewitness--you can testify as a participant. God will use your testimony to reveal more of himself to you while simultaneously using your testimony to reveal himself to others through you.

Describing the kingdom of God can be almost as challenging as receiving revelation. The reason for this seemingly insurmountable challenge is that the kingdom of God is simply beyond compare. When you consider that the kingdom of heaven is really God's way of operating and doing business, it can really overwhelm your mind. The prophet Isaiah says it best in the book that bears his name in 55:8-9: "'My thoughts are nothing like your thoughts,' says the LORD. 'And my ways are far beyond anything you could imagine. For just as the heavens are higher than the earth, so my ways are higher than your ways and my thoughts higher than your thoughts'" (NLT). The Lord makes it very clear through Isaiah that His thoughts are not even in the same realm as ours. He makes this same declaration regarding His ways. As we continue our journey to believe God, we must be willing to modify our mind-set. Clearly we are incapable of thinking as God thinks or acting as God acts. He knows our shortcomings and has made provision for every inadequacy.

In Philippians chapter 2:5 Paul writes, "Let this mind be in you, which was also in Christ Jesus." This is a very clear submissive process of the believer, allowing the mind of Christ to penetrate our minds. We must be willing to allow God to influence our thinking to the point that our thoughts become more than what we think--our thoughts become what we see. What we see or believe will ultimately become our reality. Paul goes on in Philippians 4:8 to define what should be the intentional object of our thoughts: "And now, dear brothers and sisters, one final thing. Fix your thoughts on what is true, and honorable, and right, and pure, and lovely, and admirable. Think about things that are excellent and worthy of praise" (NLT). Having the right kind of mind and thoughts requires an intentional direction of our thinking. You literally have to force yourself to think about the right things. Failure to do so causes self-fulfilling prophecy syndrome. When the majority of your thoughts are negative, you circumstances will follow the lead of your thoughts. On the other hand, when your thought life is positive and believing God, your circumstances must surrender to what you believe.

Basically we as believers must be willing to grasp the concept that God's operation exceeds our understanding. There will be many times when you believe God but may not necessarily understand Him. For example, in the Book of Jonah we find the very familiar story of Jonah, who is running from his godly duty and has an encounter with a big fish. He is thrown overboard by the mariners to an almost certain death, but he ends up being swallowed up by a big fish. The fish serves not only as Jonah's temporary residence for three days, but it also serves as his deliverance. Honestly, this makes no biological sense. I don't understand how a man could survive in the belly of a big fish for three days. I don't understand it, but I do believe it. I believe it because God said it. My understanding of the detailed "how" is not necessary for Jonah's deliverance. All that really matters is that I believe God's thoughts on the situation. God is not bound by the limitation of man's thinking.

As we continue on this journey of believing God, we must be willing to operate in faith and not necessarily on understanding. Your movements must be based on what God says in His Word, believing He will do just what He said. Don't abort your deliverance by declaring, "I just can't understand how this is going to happen." No, you may understand it, but you can still see it. You can see it because God said it! As a result, you are willing to watch for what you already saw. You must believe it because God promised it, not because it makes sense.

On this journey your faith will increase as your word intake increases and your experience increases. As your faith increases, it becomes your obligation to build the kingdom. As believers we help each other to grow as we share our experiences. God has put something in us that causes us to find comfort in commonality. When we know someone personally who has overcome obstacles, experienced faith victories, or been delivered, we can more easily relate to him or her and find hope for our situation. We build the kingdom of God when we share our kingdom experiences to provide hope for others.

There is no room for selfishness in the kingdom of God. Too many times we have well-intentioned ignorant believers. They don't mean any harm in their selfish approach to believing God, but in their self-pleasing faith they cause harm to others. When you make the blessings all about you, you miss the "all about God's kingdom" principle. Yes, God wants you to be abundantly blessed. Yes, God has offered believers exclusive access to His benefits. But you must remember what Jesus said in Luke 19:10: "The Son of man is come to seek and to save that which was lost." The purpose of Jesus coming from heaven to earth was to save those who were lost. The blessings of God are a by-product of the salvation of God.

Finally, as we continue believing God and building the kingdom of God, one final kingdom principle comes into focus. This is called the "kingdom productivity" principle. In its simplest form it can best be defined like this: there will always be productivity in the kingdom of God. Productivity could expand to include harvest. Wherever kingdom building is taking place, there will be a harvest. There are a few accompanying components required for this harvest.

First, the believer must live in accordance with God's plan for his or her life. We will go into greater detail about this in the next chapter, but obedience leads to harvest. As our focus here is building the kingdom, we must understand the harvest purpose concept. This concept is simply understanding that God blesses you with a harvest and that your harvest is a dual-purpose harvest. Your harvest is purposed to benefit you, but it's also intended to bless the body of Christ. When your harvest blesses the body of Christ, your harvest also builds the kingdom.

God will use blessings from your harvest to share His love with others. That expression of love can many times serve as the entry point of kingdom revelation. When believers see God working and blessing, they are more willing to become engaged in the kingdom-building process. Although it would seem to be the natural progression for believers to share the wealth, so to speak, it is not always that simple. When a person has struggled for a long time and finally gets some relief, human nature can easily take over with unintentional selfishness. This is a natural reaction to self-preservation. As we experience faith growth, we must understand that God wants to bless more than just us. Many times He will support our shortcomings through the abundance He has provided others. So we need to fully understand that the kingdom productivity principle is not an "all about me" solution.

As a closing thought to this chapter, I would like to briefly visit the seed concept. It basically states that how much you sow is how much you reap. Or better stated, the size of the seed determines the size of the harvest. Without getting too deep here, I just want to give you a brief thought. The determining factor in the size of the harvest is not how big a seed was sown. The real determining factor of harvest size is how the seed was sown. Was the seed sown in obedience and wrapped in faith? A faith-wrapped, obedient seed will perform well beyond its natural ability. Why is that? It is because God is not moved by your amount of seed but by your amount of faith. Your faith will cause you to be obedient. When you are full of faith and obedience, you are able to experience the "exceeding abundantly above" Ephesians 3:20 power of God. I am not suggesting that you should give less. I am simply suggesting that if you obey God in your sowing and use what God gives you for kingdom building, you will experience the "exceeding abundantly above" power of God! Build the kingdom.

Purposed To Possess The Land

Have you ever asked yourself the question "Why am I here?" It's one that often perplexes believers, indicating a personal desire to gain insight into the reason for one's existence. The challenge goes even deeper when one question leads to another. When we overlay the desire to find purpose in our effort to believe God, we can find ourselves entering a completely different level of confusion. As we have sought to understand our purpose for believing God, we have traveled through various levels of exploration, from our purpose of sharing Christ to our purpose of building the Kingdom.

Now let's take a look at our purpose from the perspective of how God has purposed us. When we consider God's purpose for us, then believing God becomes a process of accessing what God has prepared for His purposed children. Believing God requires us to attach our faith to God's promises to facilitate a transfer from faith to manifestation.

First let's take a look at who I am and why I am here. I am a creation of God with a far bigger purpose than just occupying space on the planet. I have been uniquely gifted for the service of God. In the previous chapter we dealt largely with the Kingdom and how God operates in His domain. When we look at purpose, it becomes the role we play in the Kingdom. Remember: every believer has been equipped with spiritual gifts to serve the body of Christ. Is that the end of your spiritual experience? Are we simply here to serve God and serve each other? No, being restricted to service would be far too limiting to the omnipotence of God. While our journey will never be maximized without service, we can certainly minimize our experience by offering service without experiencing participation.

God is so wise, loving, and caring that He always makes provision for His children to have a personal experience with Him. From the very beginning of making a personal decision to enter into a personal relationship with Him, we see our relationship with Christ is genuinely intimate and personal. What would a personal experience be without some personal benefits? God desires to bless each individual to walk in his or her destiny and experience Him at a personal, life-changing level. In 1 Corinthians 2:9 Paul writes, "Eye hath not seen, nor ear heard, neither have entered into the heart of man, the things which God hath prepared for them that love him." This passage clearly identifies that God has prepared some "things" for those who love Him. When you love God, there are some purposed things reserved for you personally. Now the question becomes--How do I identify these things? How do I possess these things? In Numbers 14:24 Moses records, "My servant Caleb has a different attitude than the others have. He has remained loyal to me, so I will bring him into the land he explored. His descendants will possess their full share of that land" (NLT). You have heard the phrase "Attitude is everything." While I am not sure where this phrase originated, it has great application when looking to possess the land. Dictionary.com defines *attitude* as "manner, disposition, feeling, position, etc., with regard to a person or thing; tendency or orientation, especially of the mind." The above scripture identifies Caleb as one who had a different attitude than the others. Caleb's attitude or disposition was based on what he believed God said and would deliver. When you possess a negative attitude, you will never possess the land. A negative attitude has to omit faith from its consideration in order to exist. Ironically, negativity comes with a high expectation for the worst outcome. If you are believing God to possess the land, you must have a positive attitude of faith. This must be expressed through following God fully and receiving God's promises--and ultimately you must possess the land.

Let's explore following God fully. As a general rule, there is only a small percentage of the population who ever scratch the surface of engaging to their full potential. While I am sure there are many reasons for this, certainly laziness and fear are near the top of the list. People who achieve greatness don't do it because they sit around waiting for things to happen, and they certainly do it while being afraid to move. There must be something inside you motivating you to push toward your destiny. Many people who pursue greatness often use external forms of motivation. They desire to be the best, or they want to do it for their mother or other family members. While these certainly can be motivational, the most successful people have found something within as the driving force for their greatness. As believers seeking to believe God, that something within comes from Christ and is fueled by faith, purpose, and destiny.

If we are ever to possess the land, we must fully follow God. When you fully follow God, a different spirit is required. The spirit of a person refers to the part of him or her that is sensitive and responsive to God. The spirit of a person can also reference the attitude or soul. We will use this later for the purposes of this discussion. Each human is a three-part being. Each is a being who lives in a body and has a soul. The soul houses the person's mind, will, and emotions. This part formulates the in-dividual's attitude, work ethic, and faithfulness. It is this part of the person that makes decisions. One of the biggest challenges for a person is to believe what he or she says and produce evidence to support this belief. In other words, what an individual says he or she believes and what the person does must agree. If you are going to possess the land, you can't just speak faith and not act or walk in faith. There must be conversation/action agreement. If you are going to follow God fully, you are going to have to do more than just say it.

Your daily disciplines must be clearly in step with the word, plan, and order of God. This requires a personal conviction that God is God and that His word is true. God has clear plans for you, and you believe the plans enough to take whatever steps necessary to go get what He has identified as yours. This attitude is based on conviction and not convenience. Are God's promises true? Have you been chosen by God to possess the land? If you answered yes to the above questions, you must have a determined spirit to possess according to God's plans.

Now before you get all gung ho and take off running through the door to possess the land, take a moment to consider that there is an adversary who has no interest in sitting idly by while you go possess the land. Just as God has a plan for you to possess the land, the enemy has a plan to stop you. The enemy's plan includes strategically placing obstacles in your path to trip you up. These obstacles could easily be considered deception through smoke and mirrors. The real tactic of the enemy is to get you to buy into the belief that the obstacles are too big to overcome. If he can get you to focus on the obstacles and not the outcome desired by God, he has literally enlisted you as a part of his team to help you defeat yourself.

On this journey of believing God, you must overlook obstacles by keeping your eyes on the promises of God. Don't be distracted by the smoke and mirrors. Look through the smoke and focus on the promise. Don't let your eyes deceive you. Sometimes to possess the land you have to focus on the vision God showed you and not what you see with your natural eyes. I know your obstacles appear real to you and you feel that you are in an "I have no other options" position, but a determined disciple always focuses on what God said. That is how Caleb was different. Caleb saw the obstacle of the giants in the land, but he put his focus on God's promise that they were to possess the land.

Don't let what you see or what others say get you off track. When someone else can't see what God has shown you, don't let that person talk you out of what his or her faith can't see. Many times destinies are never reached because believers are trying to drag people somewhere God didn't promise them they could go. Do not let your fear of traveling alone cause you to come short of God's promises in your life. Don't let someone else's fear stop your progress. Remember: you have to have a different spirit to possess the land.

One of the biggest reasons that believers will not walk in their purpose is that they simply refuse to receive God's promises. Additionally, one reason some are unwilling to receive God's promises is that they don't understand the process of a God promise. Believers tend to look at a promise as a future event. Promise manifestation is based on the tangible delivery of the promise and not the declaration of the promise. Although the order described above makes logical sense, it's just not how God operates. God *prepares* the promise before He *declares* the promise. In other words, God prepares the meal before He ever invites you to dinner. So by the time you hear the promise, it has already been prepared.

Now this is where your perspective must change. When pursuing God for His promises, you don't need to ask Him to make it happen, because He has *already* made it happen. You just need to apply your faith to access what already exists! The land was already promised and purposed for the children of Israel. Caleb simply believed what God said and was willing to access what was already prepared for them. That must become the believer's approach. There are no random blessings. God is not random--He is strategic. Just as you are not a random thought from God, you are purposed and specific. God has a plan with your name on it, and your plan is customized with your promises. Your promises are not connection based--they are God orchestrated. We will talk more about this in the upcoming chapters.

Please be aware of relying on earthly connections to deliver God promises. It can be far too easy to get caught up in the "building a network" frenzy. The goal here is not to minimize the power of connection but rather to appropriate the power of focusing on God's delivery system. Keep in mind that God is both the keeper and the deliverer of His promise. As a point of caution, be leery of people who try to hold their power and influence over your head. Although God does use people to deliver, it is God who uses them and not the people themselves using God. God is always in charge of His promises for you. Only He can bring to you what belongs to Him. No one has authority to direct God's promises. He alone is the orchestrator and the delivery mechanism for His promises.

The only one capable of stopping a God delivery is you. God will never halt His delivery to you unless you are unwilling to sign for the delivery of promise. I know you may be thinking, *Why would a person stop a God-promised delivery in his or her life?* The brakes are usually put on the God delivery through fear or laziness. When you are believing God, you can't be afraid to receive what He has purposed for you. When you activate the excuse system, you will put your God delivery on hold. Thoughts and statements that reference your ability or capacity will shut down your God delivery every time. Statements such as, "I can't," "I'm not ready," or "This is too much" will ultimately cause your delivery to be stifled by your fear. Don't be afraid to believe that God has purposed you to possess the land.

At all costs, please avoid the deadly disease of laziness. Life is far too short to waste time being lazy. God has given us a dash between two dates to live out our purpose. We cannot afford to waste minutes, hours, days, weeks, months, or even years due to laziness. Now I am not suggesting that we live a life out of balance that excludes adequate rest and relaxation, but I am suggesting that we don't rest and relax more than we maximize our potential.

When growing up, our children had only one real rule in our house--take care of business first. We encouraged them to have fun, enjoy life and friends, travel, and make the most of this life. However, the order was business before pleasure. When you take care of business first, you are better able to afford the costs of pleasure. Don't let laziness rob you of your God experience! God has great things in store for you, but it is up to you to receive His promise and know that you were purposed to possess the land.

Once you have the right spirit to receive God's promises, now it is time to possess the land. Possessing the land goes beyond your walking in your purpose. When you possess the land, you begin to position yourself to leave a legacy. God never intended for blessings to be for only one generation. Blessings are intended to be generational, passing from one generation to the next until He returns. A very relevant example can be found in viewing modern-day families who are known for their wealth. It seems that when someone cracks the code on obtaining sustainable wealth, the family becomes a perpetual family of wealth. Quite simply, it is human nature to desire to make life easier for your family, so you transfer to them the secret once you have it.

The first step in truly possessing the land is the stewardship of God's promises granted to you. When God blesses you, you are covenant-bound to be a good steward and manage well what God has delivered to you. Keep in mind that what God has delivered to you still belongs to Him. You are simply working with what God has blessed you with. When He blesses you, He expects increase and a return on His assets. It's much like the parable found in Matthew 25:14-30 of the master who went away on a journey and left three of his servants with talents. He left one servant five, another servant two, and the last servant one. Upon the master's return each servant was required to give an account of what he did with the talent he received. As the story proceeds, the servants who were given five and two talents doubled what they were given. The servant with one talent secured the talent but did not increase it. Servant one and two were blessed while servant three was cursed.

We have but a short window to work with the promises of God in our lives, and if we are to foster a generational blessing, we must be faithful so we can leave a legacy. The real keys are being good stewards of God's promises and keeping them in His care. This will ensure that we have a legacy of operating to our capacity in Christ beyond the present generation. How you handle the promises of God in your life reaches beyond just you. There is a generation following, and they are depending on you to learn how to possess the land.

The final key to possessing the land is to recognize that you are purposed to possess the land now. Stop waiting for some future manifestation to allow yourself to experience what God has purposed for you. Don't miss the blessing of the "now land" while looking forward to the Promised Land. Every day God is blessing you to experience Him at an unprecedented level. Your land is a "today land." That's right--you have taken time to make this personal, and you have invested to learn the purpose of believing God, so now is the time to possess your purpose. Stop waiting and go get your promise! Enjoy your victory now! You are purposed to possess the land.

Order My Steps

As we make our final transition in the book, "Believing God from a Positional Perspective," we should find ourselves once again transitioning to yet another level of faith. When seeking to believe God, your position is key. By *position* I mean where you are located in the relationship. In this final trimester of the book we will uncover where the believer should be positioned in his or her Christ relationship. Let's dig in and go a little deeper as we find favor believing God.

In Psalm 37:23 the scripture states, "The steps of a [good] man are directed and established by the Lord when He delights in his way [and He busies Himself with his every step]" (AMPC). David writes this very revealing passage regarding the position of a believer. There are two key points we need to explore before going any further. First, David says, "The steps of a good man are ordered by the Lord." Here David is letting us know beyond a reasonable doubt who is calling the shots. He does not identify God as some sideline kind of God. He does not portray God as some type of on-demand bystander waiting to answer your every call. No, David says in no uncertain terms that the Lord orders the steps of believers. So *positional belief* means you must be willing to be led by God to be in perfect position to believing God. Second, in this verse David goes on to say, "He delights in his way." This text is not referencing the believer delighting in the way of the Lord but actually the opposite. David is saying that when the Lord is ordering your steps and you are following, *the Lord* delights in, or finds pleasure in, every step you take. It pleases God when you are allowing Him to lead you!

So the only position for a believer to find real faith success is from a place of being exactly where God has led him or her. Have you ever found yourself wandering through a situation, contemplating your next move, but not really knowing how you ended up there in the first place? You may remember making a decision, but the next move was more of a reaction or a response to some circumstance--and now you find yourself in dire straits somewhere. This scenario is far too common in the life of believers. We think we have it all figured out until we look up and things just aren't working out.

Growing up as a boy, I spent some time living on the East Coast. While there I had many opportunities to visit the beaches up and down the coast. Being a young fellow, I knew how to swim but had no ocean experience. I can remember standing in water to my ankles, feeling the cold waves crashing up to my knees; this was very exhilarating. It quickly turned to anxiety when the water from the shore rushed back out to sea. They call the strong current of water rushing back out to the sea the undertow, which can be strong enough to pull you out into the ocean if you're not paying attention.

Life happens in much the same manner for believers. We move from decision to decision with little thought. We enjoy the exhilaration of life, but we are not paying attention to the undertow. Before you know it you are no longer in control, and your exhilaration becomes anxiety. How can believers combat this feeling of anxiety? We have to change our position! Our steps must be ordered by the Lord, not orchestrated by us. Order ultimately requires focus. How can believers keep a strong focus while attempting to allow God to order their steps? The answer is not simple, but it is certain; avoid getting distracted by others, remain disciplined in your walk, and be determined to reach your destination.

When God is ordering your steps, your understanding of the process is key. To receive orders from the Lord, the believer's ears must be Spirit sensitive. Romans 8:14 tells us, "As many as are led by the Spirit of God, they are the sons of God." This scripture adds some clarity to the process. The leading of God's people is delivered by the Spirit of God. When you are out of tune with the Spirit of God, there is no way you can receive clear instruction from God. Keep in mind that the Holy Spirit resides on the inside of believers, and He is there to lead you to all truth. Focus is so important, because lack of it causes you to lose sight of your ultimate goal of believing God.

In the previous chapter I noted that one of the enemy's number-one tactics to destroy the believer's faith is to enlist the support of the believer for the sole purpose of robbing him or her of God's promises and ultimately defeating the believer. Another subtle tactic of the enemy is to use other people to distract the believer. When we focus on others, there is no way we can keep our eyes on the prize. Paul makes it very clear in Ephesians 6:12, "We wrestle not against flesh and blood, but against principalities, against powers, against the rulers of the darkness of this world, against spiritual wickedness in high places." Our enemy is not each other! The enemy wants to separate believers from God at all costs. What better way for the enemy to reach his primary objective than to use the body of Christ to destroy itself through civil war? If the enemy can get us to turn on each other, we effectively cause our "already-defeated enemy" to become victorious.

People distractions are intended to derail the believer. The enemy doesn't require the believer to have a catastrophic turn of events to find success with his strategy. Distractions can be very subtle. Just a small shift in one direction can cause the believer to miss his or her target. Many times the believer has drifted off course but is unaware of the drift. The drift moves him or her off course just enough to where the drifting is not noticed until the target is missed. Don't make the mistake of ignoring the minor shift by deceiving yourself into believing you can successfully manage the minor shift. Don't allow lack of focus to cause you to be overcome by the drift. Keep your eyes focused on your course. Others may not be able to see your course, understand your course, or even respect you course. And for that reason, don't allow others to distract you from your course!

Your delight or satisfaction is not determined by another's doubt. Your delight must remain in Christ as He orders your steps. So make sure you don't paint some "picturesque Picasso" of your personal desires, wrapped up in a false sense of faith, and call it what God has ordained. As a believer, your delight is determined by your orders. God will lead you according to His will, by His Spirit, and for His glory. Just because it looks good to you doesn't mean it's for you. God specializes in customized blessings. Let Him determine what is good in your life. Let Him be right while you are wrong, giving Him room to lead and correct you while He blesses you.

While people are deliberately attempting to distract believers along their journey, others are not the most lethal weapon of the enemy. As described earlier, we can be our own worst nightmares. A major area of failure in the life of the believer is maintaining a disciplined walk. By *disciplined walk* I am suggesting that there is a given doctrine the believer is taught. This discipleship sets the standard for the believer's actions or walk. So a disciplined walk is keeping the standard prescribed by your doctrine. For the believer the doctrine is the Holy Bible.

Many believers veer off course because they are too busy trying to keep the "rules" of God. While keeping rules is a very important part of discipline, it would be limiting to stop your discipline at the point of just keeping the rules--if you fully understand them. The rules of God's doctrine go beyond just being a "good" Christian. The doctrine of God also gives the believer confidence of what God will do as well. God has established as a part of His doctrine His Service Level Agreement (SLA). The benefits of serving God are so beyond the believer's ability to grasp. In Ephesians 3:20-21 Paul makes this fact abundantly clear as he concludes his prayer for the church at Ephesus: "Now unto him that is able to do exceeding abundantly above all that we ask or think, according to the power that worketh in us, Unto him be glory in the church by Christ Jesus throughout all ages, world without end. Amen." Not to oversimplify the process, but God is able to do beyond our wildest imagination. Moreover, He does the unimaginable through believers. This is a part of the SLA of God. He will do beyond what believers think, and He will do it through believers as long as He gets the glory!

For this reason believers of God must depend on Him. When the natural mind is not even able to conceive, let alone believe, what all God can do, the believer must learn to depend on Him. Now that may not be as simple as it sounds because of how God actually guides. He rarely gives the full details of any plan He has for the believer. Sure, God gives a vision of where He's leading, but usually the vision doesn't come with step-by-step orders. God leads along a series of steps that often appear to be random or in no connecting order at all. He orders the believer's steps without giving full disclosure to the purpose of the next move. He requires a disciplined walk that depends solely on His provision. God's desire is for believers to stay the course.

Every believer would like a challenge-free journey. However, that is not a realistic expectation. Even when a believer lives a disciplined life, there is simply no way to avoid all crises. He or she will undoubtedly face difficulties along the way. Things are not always going to go the way he or she planned. God's plans always supersede those of the believer. In God's sovereignty and His perfect plan, He has a built-in recovery plan for believers. Believe it or not, God considers our humanness in His plan. He knows the frailty of the believer's emotions. He knows the believer will miss the mark. It may come as a surprise to the believer when he or she realizes the reality of his or her imperfections and inability to stay the course--but God is never caught off guard by the believer's limitations. Proverbs 24:16 says, "The godly may trip seven times, but they will get up again. But one disaster is enough to overthrow the wicked" (NLT). In God's perfect plan, or His SLA, though we fall we will not be destroyed. The believer must never allow the sting of the fall to stagnate the order process. There is no time for pity parties, doubt, and apathy. Believers must get back up! If you are going to believe God, you have to get up, allow God to clean you up, and keep moving.

There is neither room nor time to stop and blame others or blame yourself while standing outside your blessing. The believer must be determined to make it to his or her destination. Keep in mind that the destination is determined by the God order. God has a place predestined for every believer. This is one thing all believers have in common--all ultimately have the same destination. As believers we are not going separate directions for a multitude of purposes. No, God is singular in purpose. In 2 Corinthians 5:19 we read, "God was in Christ, reconciling the world to himself, no longer counting people's sins against them. And he gave us this wonderful message of reconciliation" (NLT). Every believer must understand that all roads of God lead to reconciliation with God. For this reason

God will always lead believers to himself. This is really wonderful news. When God orders the believer's steps, the believer has a security and certainty that He is the final destination.

This is the assistance the believer needs to facilitate an unshakeable determination to reach his or her goal. Knowing God is leading the believer to himself should serve as a peace-provider--even while in a storm. God is incapable of conflicted leadership. He will never get confused and lead believers to do anything that separates them from their ultimate destination, which is Jesus Christ. There are countless erroneous testimonies (and I use the term loosely) of God leading individuals to commit sin as some form of test of their faith. There will be times when a believer sins, but the credit for those committed sins must rest on the shoulders of the believer and not God. The failure comes when the believer chooses of his or her own free will to respond to the enemy's temptation by engaging in sin. A God test will never lead the believer to separate himself or herself from Him. First Corinthians 10:13 says, "The temptations in your life are no different from what others experience. And God is faithful. He will not allow the temptation to be more than you can stand. When you are tempted, he will show you a way out so that you can endure" (NLT). This scripture paints a very clear picture of the antidote for sin, which is the faithfulness of God. When believing God the process must be clear. Believers must believe in the faithfulness of God. Even in times of trouble, God is faithful. As He is leading believers to himself, He must remain faithful to them to protect them from a sin destruction that would be certain to overtake troubled would-be believers if not for Christ.

Finally, believers must keep their eyes on God! No matter what comes, if God is to order the believer's steps, the believer must stay focused. In Matthew 14 Peter was faced with the opportunity to trust God to walk on water or lose focus and drown. Believers must keep their focus on God--because God is the holder of their inheritance. He has an inheritance in store for every believer. Inheritance becomes reality when believers are willing to keep their focus on God. Don't get caught looking to the left or to the right, but keep your eyes on the prize of God!

God has promises for the believer. The key to believing God is to know that the believer's steps are ordered by the Lord. In the order of God believers find the inheritance of God. In the inheritance of God believers find their way to possessing the promises of God. So as you believe God, make it a personal process. In this personal process, allow God to lead you to the place of your blessing. God is leading, but are you following? Have you allowed your intellect to outweigh your faith? Are you using popular phrasing while abandoning active faith in your life? Be willing to make the adjustment to getting behind the Lord, and He will lead you into all truth. He will lead you according to His will. He will lead you to the land He promised you!

Deliver Us

Many believers in God often find themselves in some precarious predicaments. With the challenges of life, family, and ministry, sometimes life can feel as if the tail were wagging the dog. The believer is being slung from here to there, seemingly having no control of his or her own life. Questions such as "How did I end up here?" or "Am I ever going to catch a break?" coupled with statements like "I'm just doing the best I can" become the order of the day. It can really be overwhelming when believers feel they are stuck or even held captive by the trials of life.

Such believers feel they are actually living for God and believing God--but are not making any progress. It is as if they feel God has somehow forsaken them or doesn't hear them when they call. This can be so frustrating. It is one thing for believers to know they are out of step with God. They realize they haven't been as close to the Lord as they should be, so they understand the problems they are facing and attribute them to their own personal shortcomings. However, when that is not the case, they find themselves disheartened by their painful condition. Just imagine Christians who believe that everything is as it should be. Their spiritual life is in order. They have an active Bible study, they worship regularly and pray daily--but they still find themselves struggling with the same sin, setbacks, and disappointments as a regular course of life. How does a believer stay strong in the fight? How does he or she refrain from just giving up and throwing in the towel? How does a believer find the strength to endure the painful bondage?

In this chapter we will take an in-depth look at the process a disciple must endure to be delivered. This process of being delivered requires the individual to be transitioned from captivity to liberty. In previous chapters we noted that a disciple is a student who requires a teacher, who follows a given doctrine. In the believer's life the Holy Bible is the doctrine. This fact cannot be up for discussion. The Bible is the source document and the doctrinal guide for living. The Bible does not require a supporting document. The Bible can and does stand alone in its validity as the Word of God. The disciple must not be unstable or uncertain on this. The fact of the Bible's authority is not debatable for those who would believe God. The disciple must accept the Bible as one-hundred-percent true. Having clearly and definitively established the Bible as the source document and guide for believers, let's explore more deeply the practicality of biblical living for the disciple.

Unfortunately there is a myth running rampant through modern-day religion that believers in God are somehow exempt from trouble, lack, doubt, or fear. The religious society has decided to question the faith of those who experience what is commonly referred to as "life." This is where the confusion comes in regarding an authentic faith experience. Somehow performance has been determined as the quantifier for blessings. Essentially the better one performs, the more blessed he or she is. I am not suggesting that performance is insignificant, but I am suggesting that "religious performance" is not the driver to living a stress-free life. There is no secret formula to living this life completely stress free. Make no mistake about it: believers will suffer too.

So the real question is this: How does a believer make it through challenging times? How does a believer spiritually escape the bondage and captivity of life? How can a believer go from just saying, "I'm delivered," "I'm healed, "I'm free," to experiencing deliverance, healing, and liberty? This delivered reality is attained through the disciple's proper following of the doctrine of the Bible. When God's order is followed, deliverance will come.

In Matthew 6:13 we find these words as a lesson from Jesus: "And lead us not into temptation, but deliver us from evil: For thine is the kingdom, and the power, and the glory, for ever. Amen." Although this prayer is commonly referred to as "The Lord's Prayer," it could really be better identified as "The Disciple's Prayer." In this verse Jesus is actually teaching the disciples how they ought to pray. While we could really go deeply here, my goal is to simply deal with a few nuggets regarding deliverance. The disciple is clearly instructed here to request God not to lead him or her into a place to be tempted. One of the simplest ways to be delivered is to avoid the temptation or the need to be delivered altogether. Many times believers find themselves in distant places from God due to disobedience to God.

Jesus goes on to teach the disciples to pray, "But deliver us from evil". Here He teaches His disciples to seek protection from temptation and deliverance from evil. Seems simple enough, right? Well, if it were that simple, I am sure no believer would ever be tempted or trapped and held in bondage. If the believer is to find success on this journey of believing God, he or she must learn how to live according to the deliverance formula. I am sure you are asking, "What formula?" The formula requires that the disciple desire leadership, deal with temptation, and depend on deliverance.

As previously discussed, the disciple is a student or a learner. One of the most important keys to discipleship is the desire of the disciple to be led. There are so many facets wrapped up in the point of the disciple's willingness to be led. One of the most challenging things a believer will face is the challenge of submission. So many believers lose it at the point of submission. Submission is by definition a willingness to voluntarily place yourself under the authority of another. The real bottom line of the definition involves the believer willingly surrendering control to another.

Now it is quite understandable why believers find it so challenging to submit to each other. Clearly, the process of submitting to one another basically suggests that the believer is placing himself or herself in a position of leadership under the authority of a flawed peer. No one wants to surrender control to another person. Although the challenge of personal submission may have some "fleshly" merit, it clearly contradicts scripture. In Ephesians 5:21 it is clear that Christians are expected to submit to one another: "submitting yourselves one to another in the fear of God." This expectation when forced to stand on its own merit can be very difficult to process. Our process as believers is to choose obedience over managing a process.

The irony in this submission process is that believers view submission to God much in the same manner that they view submission to people. I'm not saying believers see people and God in the same vein. I am saying believers offer the same point of view regardless of who or what they are submitting to. As a result, people must move their view of submission to a godly perspective over a selfish position. When a disciple desires leadership, he or she is demonstrating a willingness to submit. Many times the believer is asking God for something but actually has no idea of how it works or what the associated costs are. When you ask God to lead, just by the question you are suggesting to God that you are ready to follow. The believer's readiness to follow is the first step in being delivered.

Furthermore, asking God to lead is really an indication that you have no idea where you are going. This can be very difficult for believers to admit. This ties back to some false sense that believers are in control of their lives in the first place. God is often looked at as an "in case of emergency only" God. So believers feel some sort of exposure of vulnerability when placed in a position to believe God.

In much this same manner, believers struggle with admitting they are ever lost. It's much like the man and his wife who are driving around as the man has too much pride to admit to his wife that he is lost. As the wife holds the global positioning system (GPS) device, listening to the step-by-step instructions the kind voice on the other end is offering, she offers these same kind instructions to her loving husband--but he won't or can't accept the directions because he "isn't lost." Many believers dwell in bondage simply because they are unwilling to admit they are lost. When disciples desire leadership, they are admitting that they are willing to submit and are also admitting they are lost.

Ultimately, the admission of a desire for leadership and an admission of being lost demonstrate an acknowledged dependency on God. God dependency could be better defined as a trust or reliance on God. No matter what a believer is facing, big or small, their answer is the same--take it to the Lord. This seems to be automatic, but there is something innate in the human mind that suggests they are able to handle things on their own. Believing God is not an event but rather a lifestyle of total reliance on God in every situation. Believers cannot have different situational problem-solving tools depending on the situation. Many times believers look to others' willingness to participate in the process as a restriction or encumbrance to God's ability to work in a given situation. In other words, they may not execute their own responsibilities because they feel it won't really matter anyway. They feel that in this way they have empowered other people who are unwilling to seek God from their side of the fence to perform their task. A believer's dependence on God means doing what God requires of him or her no matter what another person does, all the while believing God to work it out. In spite of what others say or do, do not allow another's faith, commitment, and action to deter you from believing God enough to do whatever He leads you to do.

In order to be delivered, the believer must also deal with temptation. James 1:13-14 states, "Remember, when someone wants to do wrong it is never God who is tempting him, for God never wants to do wrong and never tempts anyone else to do it. Temptation is the pull of man's own evil thoughts and wishes" (TLB). In understanding temptation the believer must know the source and method of operation for temptation. God will never tempt the believer. If He were to tempt the believer and the believer were to fail, it would mean God put the believer in a place to be intentionally moved away from God. God would never do that.

While God will never tempt a believer, it is important to identify who will. The enemy is at the root of temptation but does not have the power to tempt believers. In referencing James 1:14 we find that what really tempts a person is his or her own evil thoughts and wishes. When believers are struggling with temptation, they are really fighting an internal fight. The things they possess in their own hearts are what causes them to fall. The enemy simply uses believers' own lusts against them. They must somehow find a way to deal with the dirt on the inside if they are ever going to find success fighting the temptation demon.

Following God is a sure way for believers to avoid the temptation trap. Although following God does not remove all temptation for the believer, it greatly reduces the power of temptation. When following God, the believer can be assured that He will never lead them to a place of captivity or bondage. God will not put a believer in a position to fail. Even when the believer finds himself or herself in a position of temptation, this is not new to God. First Corinthians 10:13 says, "The temptations in your life are no different from what others experience. And God is faithful. He will not allow the temptation to be more than you can stand. When you are tempted, he will show you a way out so that you can endure" (NLT). God actually protects the believer from temptation--not to the point at which the believer won't experience temptation but rather to the point at which the believer will have both an exit strategy and an endurance strategy. God will provide what he or she needs to endure and get away from temptation. In this process God is glorified because He has kept those who believe in Him.

Resistance is really contingent upon the believer's willingness to deal with temptation. If a believer who is willing to be led by Christ will seek to resist the temptation, he or she will be delivered. Whether it is through the believer's God strength or the God-navigated escape route, there is a way to make it through temptation. God has ready-made protection plans, but their implementation is left to the disciple who is believing God. Stop giving the enemy all the credit for overtaking you. God has provided deliverance for you. Stay the course, and watch God do wonderful things in your life.

The disciple must depend on God for deliverance. Keep in mind that deliverance is necessary only when one is being held captive or in bondage. There is no need for deliverance when a believer is walking in liberty. Deliverance rescues believers from the enemy. To quickly revisit the topic, a believer can be held captive by the enemy only when he or she assists the enemy in the process. Believers are taken captive by the enemy only when they aide the enemy to take them captive while being unaware of the enemy's tactics. It is primarily the believer's willingness to yield to temptation that places him or her in bondage. God always comes through for those who belong to Him.

This is the assurance only believers possess. God will come and deliver those who belong to Him. In the book of Daniel 3:16-17 we read, "Shadrach, Meshach, and Abednego replied, 'O Nebuchadnezzar, we do not need to defend ourselves before you. If we are thrown into the blazing furnace, the God whom we serve is able to save us. He will rescue us from your power, Your Majesty'" (NLT). What the Hebrew boys understood was that their defense was not their responsibility but God's, and deliverance was in His hands. As believers we must begin to better understand the processes of God and operate in them. God will defend and deliver His children, but His children have to stand on His promises.

Just as Jesus taught the disciples to pray, "Deliver us from evil," modern-day believers must follow this same prescription. We have to believe God to be delivered. God intends for His children to believe Him from a delivered perspective. Believers must see themselves as delivered before they even begin to pray. The position from which God expects His children to believe Him is the position of someone under the covering of God.

Deliverance draws the believer close to God. When believers are no longer in bondage, they are intentionally closer to

God. God desires to be close to His children. He knows that the closer believers stay to Him the more authentic and rewarding relationship they can have with Him. God wants all believers to remain under His covering so they can experience Him in a real and personal way. Believe God in a personal way. Remember to always approach Him from a place of purpose, knowing that Christ is our purpose for believing God and that our position should be a position of deliverance and not that of captives. Trust that God has already set you free, and you can live in your purpose now.

As you move forward on the journey of believing God, remember: you are already in a delivered position--in Jesus' name. Amen!

Victory Is Mine

The journey of believing God must be from a position of victory and not defeat. Many times the journey of faith begins in the midst of an overwhelming challenge. Based on very difficult circumstances, would-be believers find themselves grasping at almost anything to make it through their present circumstances. Many different "faith" solutions are born out of crisis. The challenge with this methodology is that inactive faith is not easily turned on just because there is a crisis. It would be like having a tool in your garage you have never opened, never having read the manual about--and then needing that tool in an emergency situation. Although the tool is perfect for the job, it can be of no real value to the owner under such circumstances--not because the owner doesn't have access to or a right to the tool, but because he or she is not at all familiar with it. At best, the owner has seen others from a distance use such a tool, but being an eyewitness to the outcome does not make you proficient in the process of using the tool yourself. As a result, the tool designed to benefit the owner has become a source of frustration and disappointment as opposed to a key to victory over the crisis at hand.

A defeated position or a defeated mind-set works in much the same manner as it relates to believing God, rendering the power of prayer and faith inoperable. As previously discussed, access to the power of God comes only through a personal relationship with Christ. Let me reiterate--it is a personal relationship with Christ and not an encounter.

Many times would-be believers find themselves in a church setting and become overwhelmed with the emotion of the service. They also find themselves inspired by the passion of others experienced in the service. This can be very challenging for many reasons. First, an authentic relationship with Christ can at times be a very emotional experience fueled by passion. To the onlooker the immediate outflow is visible but there is no real insight given to the process.

Many times believers speak in familiar "religious" terms. While this form of communication works among believers, it can really be damaging to someone who is seeking to enter into a personal relationship with Jesus Christ. It would be similar to using slang to communicate with a person who has just learned English as a second language. The person understands English, but he or she misinterprets the slang by taking the expressions literally. As a result, would-be believers find themselves disappointed through the faith process simply because they have not learned the process of believing God from a positional perspective. Believers are to believe God from a position of victory and not defeat! The process of operating from a position of victory requires a clear understanding of the Resurrection, an understanding of the reality of redemption, and finally the process of recognition.

In 1 Corinthians 15:12-14 the apostle Paul writes, "Now if Christ be preached that he rose from the dead, how say some among you that there is no resurrection of the dead? But if there be no resurrection of the dead, then is Christ not risen: And if Christ be not risen, then is our preaching in vain, and your faith is also vain" (KJV). The very foundation of the Christian faith is the resurrection of Jesus Christ, the Son of God who came in human form to live a sinless life and die as payment for the sins of those who would believe in Him as their Savior. Now this fact comes almost as second nature to experienced believers, but it can become a real stumbling block for those who are new to Christ. When Christ is reduced to just a provider of blessings and not recognized as the Savior, the believer is in jeopardy of completely missing the power of the Resurrection.

Let's take a deeper look at the power of the Resurrection. The nature or normal way of humanity is to sin. Sin starts in a seemingly innocent fashion of basic selfishness. Basic selfishness puts the individual in a position of exclusive authority. The believer who gives in to this basically becomes the judge and jury in determining what is right and what is wrong in his or her life. It's hard to believe basic selfishness can lead to such a position of autonomy. But that is really where it all begins. Autonomy is birthed out of basic selfishness, which establishes authority. This authority hinders the dependency quotient for Christ. The key to the believer's position of victory over defeat requires dependence on the power of Christ that comes though the Resurrection. The Resurrection serves as the differentiator between Christianity and all other religions. When the believer gains a true understanding of the purpose and power of the Resurrection, then he or she is able to believe from the position of victory.

The believer is no longer limited to the power sourced through his or her basic selfishness program, which forces its participants to face their inevitable failures as a way of life that they just have to learn to live with. When people rely on themselves only, they are forced to learn how to deal with disappointment, devastation, and defeat as a way of life. The Resurrection is the remedy for this flawed, basic selfishness program way of thinking.

Why is the Resurrection so significant? Simply because it concludes the process of sin payment and Christ access. Romans 6:23 best identifies the payment requirement for sin: "The wages of sin is death; but the gift of God is eternal life through Jesus Christ our Lord." The basic selfishness program is infected with sin. Sin must be paid for. Only Jesus Christ was able to meet the requirement to pay for this sin debt. His qualification begins with His God status, going through His sinless earth-living experience and apex with His resurrection. Had Jesus not remained sinless on the earth, there would be no forgiveness of sin. Jesus' sinless living fulfilled the law, thereby giving believers access to forgiveness of sin and ultimately access to the power to live in victory!

To believe God, the individual must receive the redemption of Jesus Christ. In order to have a proper view of redemption, one must first understand where he or she once was. *Redemption* by definition indicates that there is a reclaiming of a possession once previously owned. The challenge with redemption is that although one may have been the original owner, at some point the possession and owner have been separated. In order to reclaim ownership, there is an additional transaction required to reunite the possession with its original owner. Even though the original owner paid the price for the original ownership position, a second payment must be made to reclaim the ownership position. This second payment is called *redemption*.

This is the position Christians find themselves in. God is the creator of humanity. Genesis 2:7 states, "The LORD God formed man of the dust of the ground, and breathed into his nostrils the breath of life; and man became a living soul." This passage established God as the creator of man and woman. As such, He took time to establish people--plus their purpose and provision. Just imagine: God had created the first man and woman and placed them in the garden, which God had created in order for humanity to have dominion and authority. After this, the man and his wife make an intentional decision to disobey God, thereby separating themselves from their Creator. God in His wisdom already had a redemption strategy ready. God knew people would separate themselves from Him. Matthew 1:21 tells us, "She shall bring forth a son, and thou shalt call his name JESUS: for he shall save his people from their sins." Jesus was purposed to save His people from their sins.

Sin is the culprit that separated people from God. Jesus Christ made the payment to reunite humanity with God. Practically speaking, sin appears to have regained the upper hand. Would-be believers seem to have become more comfortable with the "fact" of sin as a part of life. It seems the universal acceptance of imperfection is becoming the standard for the day. A defeated position in sin has become normalized in the life of believers. As a result, they often attempt to operate from an already-defeated mentality. Believers must consider the price Christ paid for the their redemption before waving the white flag of surrender to sin. Sin cannot be allowed to continue to drive a wedge between believers and their God-given purpose. There is no such thing as acceptable sin. All sin separates believers from God, and as a result sin must be dealt with through confession and repentance.

Sin eternally separates people from God. The only way to deal with it is to receive what God has accomplished through the death of His Son, Jesus Christ. To appreciate and value the sacrifice of Christ is not only to accept His death as payment for sin--the believer must commit to his or her Christ experience of living from a position of victory. The believer must know his or her life was mortgaged by sin, but Jesus paid the mortgage off. The payment was not just to wash away the past, but it also insured victorious living in this present life as well as eternity. While victorious living does not suggest a life without challenges, it does suggests that God will make a way in every situation in the life of the believer. Romans 8:28 says, "We know that all things work together for good to them that love God, to them who are the called according to his purpose."

The Bible is clear: not all things may be good, but they *work together* for good. This passage gives a clear understanding of how God uses everything in the life of the believer for the benefit of the believer.

It is important as believers that we are not defined by our failures. Failures do not take the victory away from us unless we fail to follow God's process of redemption to access Him in trouble. Spiritual failures require confession and repentance to become eligible for victory. Confession simply means agreeing with God as to what is right and what is wrong. Confession is not the believer's informing God of his or her wrongdoing but rather acknowledging the understanding that what he or she did was wrong in His sight. Then comes repentance, as the believer turns away from that sin and turns to God. This process is the only way believers can develop a victorious mind-set, which is based not on human perfection but rather God's perfect plan of redemption. When a believer knows for certain that Jesus has already paid for his or her sins, he or she can live in victory. Let's be clear: living in victory doesn't mean living with an acceptable amount of negligible sin. No, living in victory means that the believer receives the redemptive work of Christ and then trusts God to keep him or her from sinning.

Victorious living cannot have at its core a "sin acceptable" mind-set. Victory is often surrendered by believers, because somewhere along the way they have convinced themselves that the imperfection of humanity is a part of the package and as a result sin is normal. It is only because Jesus was willing to give His life that believers have the victorious opportunity redemption provides. Don't fall for the enemy's trap of undisciplined living. Believers should address whatever sin issues they have head-on with the confidence that Christ has already paid the price for them to live a victorious life! With Christ, believers know they have life! Stop just existing and letting life toss you here and there. The believer must thank Jesus for dying and celebrate Jesus' gift of life. Jesus is the only reason believers can live a victorious life!

Finally, believers must possess a thankful mind-set. With all Christ has done for believers, they should express unconditional gratitude. First Thessalonians 5:18 says, "In every thing give thanks: for this is the will of God in Christ Jesus concerning you." This passage is so important, because many believers operate in "situational thanksgiving," which happens when thanksgiving shows up only in positive situations. When things are working well or heading in the believer's favor, thanksgiving is in order--which is much more than situational recognition of God playing the role of genie in a bottle. Thanksgiving is not simply a holiday celebrated the fourth Thursday of November. God is an everyday God and is deserving of an *everyday* thanksgiving.

It is right for believers to recognize God with a thank-you on their journey of believing God. Thanksgiving should show up in the believer's praise. Praise in an expression of the value a believer possesses for God. On this journey of believing God, God himself has made a way for victory to become a manifestation and not just imagination. Believers owe God a praise of thanksgiving. Just consider life without Christ--there would be no victory. Life would be filled with challenge after challenge with no real hope for deliverance. But because God loves His children so much, they should stop and tell Him, "Thank you." Thanksgiving is a way of life and not simply a response to an event. Every day of the believer's life there are many reasons to recognize God with a thank-you.

The disappearance of the thank-you is no surprise. People, even believers, have forgotten how to say it. Something as simple as thanking someone for holding a door open has almost become a thing of the past. For most people who were born in the baby boomers generation (1946-1964) or generation X (1965-early 1980s) or before, manners were an essential part of their lives. Being taught to say "Please" and "Thank you" were just a part of the package. It was common practice in homes all over the United States for families to sit down together for dinner--and before anyone took a single bite, someone from the family, usually the patriarch, would thank God for providing the meal they were about to partake. It seems so simple, but believers today barely let the ink dry on the blessing before they return to their standard order of complaining.

Since believers know they have the victory, they must be willing to thank God. Remember: thanksgiving is not temporary. Thanksgiving is a way of living. The believer's way of living is the best way to tell God, "Thank you." When facing trials, tribulations, and temptation, believers must stay focused on the power of God. First Corinthians 15:58 reads, "Therefore, my beloved brethren, be ye stedfast, unmoveable, always abounding in the work of the Lord, forasmuch as ye know that your labour is not in vain in the Lord." Consistency in Christ is the best way to tell God, "Thank you." Jesus put us believers in a victorious position in our everyday living. We cannot afford to get distracted by difficult times. Steadfastness is willingness to trust God through whatever comes and keep a victorious mind-set every step of the way.

The only way believers will be able to maintain a steadfast walk is to be fixed in their faith. Yes, the believer's faith must be unshakeable. God has purposed the believer to live from a position of victory and not defeat! The believer must make up his or her mind. God is ready, willing, and able to keep His promises. Make this a personal process. Confess daily, "Victory is mine!" Take possession of your favor, thanking God along the way, and tell God, "Thank you," for keeping you in the name of Jesus. Thank you, Lord, for the victory! Victory is mine!

Show Us Your Glory

Every believer desires to witness and experience the glory of the Lord, which represents the manifestation of His power. Ultimately when a person believes God, the experience of His showing up in the middle of a believer's sincere request is every believer's pinnacle Christian experience. When he or she has struggled through circumstances and situations that have literally taken his or her hope away, when every approach to making it through these various circumstances and situations has failed miserably, a sense of desperation takes over. The challenge placed upon the believer's faith is overwhelmed with doubt and frustration. It is as this point that he or she is left to totally and completely depend on God for restoration.

The restoration that comes with answered prayer is the glory of the Lord manifested. This experience is very difficult to explain from a human perspective. There is really nothing relatable from an earthly perspective to the glory of the Lord. It shows up in a natural situation and transforms the natural to the supernatural. When a believer is pursuing God for a necessary blessing just to make it from day to day, the supernatural becomes naturally necessary. The believer gets to a place of reaching the very end of his or her rope and is now hoping against hope. He or she is looking at a lifeless situation, and only the glory of the Lord can infuse life into this broken place.

Too many times believers are not established or grounded enough in their Christian walk to understand the difference between spiritual faith and a human desire. Spiritual faith is a biblical process used to set proper expectations of God in His response to the believer's faith. While human desire can pose as faith, it is really nothing more than a believer's desperate wish for a holy God to meet a natural need. This often leads to disappointment in God and can also cause loss of confidence in Him. God's desire is for believers to experience His glory as a part of their everyday lives. He does not want them to falter in their faith due to ignorance. He wants to bless His people and deliver them into the full presence of His glory. The real key to experiencing the glory of the Lord is to know His voice, follow His instructions, and finally dwell in the His presence.

God's voice can be difficult to identify and comprehend. Many believers lose faith before their faith journey ever begins due to their inability to identify the voice of God. For Adam, God's handmade creation, the voice of God was easily identifiable. Adam and Eve literally walked in the presence of God in the garden as they dwelt with Him. Even for Moses, God spoke directly to him on Mount Sinai.

For modern-day believers the voice of God is not quite as easy to identify--or is it? How does God speak to believers? Can they hear God audibly? Does God call them by name to get their attention? Indeed, God speaks to believers in many ways. The foundation for believers today is not going to come primarily in audible form, although it remains a possibility. God may not call believers by name, but He will certainly get their attention. He speaks to them mostly through His Word. Romans 10:14 states, "How can they call on him to save them unless they believe in him? And how can they believe in him if they have never heard about him? And how can they hear about him unless someone tells them?" (NLT). So hearing about God is a prerequisite to believing God. Paul goes on to say in Romans 10:17, "So then faith cometh by hearing, and hearing by the word of God." This scripture helps to identify how God uses His Word to speak to believers. If a believer wants to really hear God, he or she must ingest His Word.

The process of believing God requires one to first hear about God. Once the person hears about Him, he or she must respond by calling on the name of the Lord to be saved (Romans 10:13). From the point of salvation, the believer must actively increase his or her ability to believe God. The process is begun by growing, reading, hearing, and living the Word of God. The believer is now in a position to declare that he or she knows God. Please keep in mind that knowing God is a lifelong process. In human form the believer will never exhaustively know everything there is to know about God. However, there are two principles that must be accepted in order to maximize one's journey of believing God.

Believers must acknowledge the sovereignty of God, recognizing that He is the supreme authority and possesses all power. Sovereignty revelation is the revelation that God is in full control. He is not governed by any higher power or any other source. God is self-existent and eternal. In Revelation 1:8 He says, "I am the Alpha and the Omega--the beginning and the end. . . . I am the one who is, who always was, and who is still to come--the Almighty One" (NLT). While conceptually this sounds good, believers stumble as it relates to truly acknowledging the sovereignty of God.

For instance, believers often give themselves too much credit or take too much blame for their life situations. Some believe they are as "blessed" simply because of how they have managed their lives. They were responsible, or they took advantage of every opportunity the Lord blessed them with. They credit themselves with being the source of their success by being a good "partner" with God--while others tend to blame themselves for their situation of difficulty and distress because they have not been good people. They take the apathetic approach of believing they somehow deserve to be in misery because of their failures. They never even expect good things from the Lord because they simply believe they don't deserve them.

While there is certainly a responsibility of believers to participate in the blessing process, they are not blessed or cursed solely based on their own participation. John 9:2-3 frames up an opportunity for the power of God to be on display: "'Rabbi,' his disciples asked him, 'why was this man born blind? Was it because of his own sins or his parents' sins?' 'It was not because of his sins or his parents' sins,' Jesus answered. 'This happened so the power of God could be seen in him'" (NLT). The man's blindness was not a curse. It was an opportunity for God's presence to be made visible. The sovereignty of God allows Him to create circumstances and conditions for the purpose of demonstrating His glory to make known who He is. It really becomes the believer's responsibility to learn to accept the will of God as he or she learns to hear the voice of God.

Accepting God's will means more than just sitting back and waiting for Him to move a mountain. Rather, it means believing Him to work in every situation the believer faces. Believers must not give up in the middle of a storm--they must continue to move forward as they are led by God. The key in being led by God is having a strong relationship with Him. The glory of the Lord is experienced only in a right relationship with Him. This relationship is not a general, from-a-distance relationship. Rather, it must be a *personal relationship.* This phrase is almost overused in the body of Christ. Many speak of *relationship,* but what does it really mean?

Relationship really addresses the connection between parties. The primary valuation of relationship is time. The strength of any relationship can really be reduced to the amount of time invested in it. Time is certainly not the only factor, but without time, relationships are unable to progress to the next level. On this journey of believing God, the believer must be willing to invest time with God to grow the relationship. Unlike earthly relationships, in which people can invest a great deal of time up front that will solidify it for a lifetime, believers must make an ongoing investment of time with the Lord to solidify their God relationship. The believer must understand his or her God relationship from this perspective; God already knows everything about the believer. There are no mysteries that require revelation for God in the relationship process of the believer's relationship with God. The real opportunity in the God-believer relationship is for the believer to spend more time with God to get to know Him better on a personal level. As he or she becomes more intimate with God, God is able to bless the believer according to His will and not according to the limitations of the believer's faith. As the believer gets to know God in a personal way, the glory of the Lord becomes more attainable.

In a more intimate relationship model, the believer begins to understand how the master/servant model works between the believer and God. In the master/servant model, the believer understands both the authority and responsibility of the master. The master's responsibility is to lead, guide, and protect the servant. The servant's responsibility is to serve the master.

On the believing-God journey, the believer operates in the role of servant and must be willing to believe God for the purpose of better serving Him. The servant's position is never to separate from the master. The servant wants to serve the master in any way he or she can. So when the master's leadership meets the servant's service, the result is a pleased master and a blessed servant. This process becomes the glory of the Lord manifested in the life of the believer.

A clear understanding of the master/servant relationship must move beyond understanding to implementation. The servant must be willing to follow the instructions of the master. Yes, there are some general master/servant rules that apply to all servants. However, with the personal relationship comes personalized instructions. God gives very specific instructions to the believer. Although the instructions may be specific, they are not necessarily given from an all-inclusive perspective. This can be very difficult for believer to comprehend.

While God's instructions are very specific, they are also given in step-by-step, sequential order, on an individual basis. God will often instruct believers on the next step only, not giving insight to the ultimate plan. This proves to be very difficult for believers. Although most could not handle God's full disclosure, they somehow believe that knowing more of what God is ultimately trying to accomplish would make it easier to follow the Master's instruction. That does sound good, but many times the believer is going to be faced with numerous trials and obstacles along the journey. These obstacles, if fully disclosed up front, may actually detour him or her from even taking the journey. He or she can't see the development that will come only when the he or she faces and overcomes the obstacle. One trial prepares the believer for the next; so he or she must trust that God is leading along the path He has customized specifically for him or her. When the believer resigns himself or herself to believing God according to His plan, the believer positions himself or herself to believe God according to His strategy and not the believer's own plans.

God's instructions are not only step-by-step, sequential, and individual--they are strategic. God uniquely gifts each believer, equipping him or her to serve the body of Christ in a very specific way. This process of equipping is a strategy-based approach. God equips according to His strategy. Remember: the believer sees God's strategy only as God gives him or her vision according to His strategy. One thing to keep in mind is the limits on the believer's ability to see, which is directly tied to his or her ability to hear God. The believer can't see what God is showing without hearing what God is telling him or her. Consequently, the believer can rarely see as far as God's personalized vision for him or her reaches. God's plans for the believer must always be the source of the believer's "believing." Participation by following instructions is critical to manifestation. Believers who want to experience exactly what God has promised them must be willing to do exactly as God instructs them to do. Remember: His instructions for believers always align with His plans for them.

Finally, if the believer is to experience the glory of the Lord, he or she must dwell in the presence of the Lord. Dictionary.com defines *dwell* as "to live or stay as a permanent resident; reside." From this definition it could be stated that the believer must be a preeminent resident in God's presence or God's dwelling place. Many times believers choose to leverage their dual citizenship for their own perceived selfish benefit. As believers, we know that there are both the earthly citizenship and the kingdom citizenship that must be considered. The earthly citizenship must deal with the flesh restrictions that accompany it. The earthly citizenship also has to deal with the flesh of others, laws of the land, and even the opposition of the enemy. Kingdom citizenship allows the believer to live in this world but not be a part of this world. There are places on earth a believer's kingdom access can override. He or she can be faced with earthly citizenship limitations while being blessed beyond the earthy restriction, because kingdom citizenship privileges supersede earthly rights.

Dwelling in the presence of God is much more than an emotional experience. While the power of God can certainly produce emotion, it is not emotion that produces the glory of the Lord. The challenge with emotion is its contagious character. Consider an individual attending the funeral of someone he or she does not know. The emotion of sadness can easily be transferred because of the emotional atmosphere, not necessarily due to the pain of loss. In much the same way, believers can participate in a highly emotional worship experience, and the emotion of the experience can be transferred without the power of God being transferred. This happens to many would-be believers. When they are faced with walking in what they "felt," they are under-equipped to do so because they have no real frame of reference for dwelling in the presence of God.

The glory of the Lord is personal and requires a personal investment. On this journey of believing God, the believer must be willing to personally invest in the Lord. Once the believer experiences the glory of the Lord, his or her life will be eternally changed! When he or she experiences the manifested presence of the glory of the Lord, there is no way he or she can remain the same. This causes many conflicts in the body of Christ, because a believer who has experienced the glory of the Lord changes in his or her spiritual walk significantly. This change often causes personal loss of friends, acquaintances, and sometimes even family. Not everyone may be able to process or accept the glory of the Lord in a believer's life. It can be frightening to someone who has never experienced it. A believer should not be surprised or alarmed by an exodus of former associates as his or her faith walk increases. Not everyone is built to go on this journey of believing God.

Let's conclude with one final thought. The believer can't rush the glory of the Lord. God has a timing that is left only for His knowing and understanding. As for believers, the key to faith is believing God for His timing and His will. Again, believers may never make it to their destiny due date if they knew exactly how long it would take. Many would possibly forfeit their destiny simply because it might take too long. Remember: God's timing allows for the believer's development. Believers can't walk in the glory of the Lord until they are mature enough to receive the glory of the Lord.

Many believers witness the glory of the Lord but don't experience the glory of the Lord. God will allow you to see what He is doing, but because of His sovereignty it may not be time for you to personally experience the glory of the Lord yet. Let "yet" be an encouragement to the believer. "Yet" simply means it is a matter of timing and not eligibility. "Yet" signifies that at the appointed time the believer will experience the glory of the Lord. Believer, be patient--there is no rushing the glory of the Lord. When the time comes, He will show you His glory! The wonderful thing about God is that He can reveal His glory to the believer without going public. Everything God has for the believer may not be for immediate public release. He will show the believer His glory personally and then at the appointed time will share with others what He has done for the individual believer--so that others may come to experience the glory of the Lord.

On this journey of believing God, remember that the glory belongs to the Lord. He alone is the producer of glory, and all believers must be willing to give the glory back to the Lord that He has already produced. Expect to see the glory of the Lord!

CONCLUSION
Believing God

As you have journeyed through this book, I pray you have been equipped and challenged to believe God from a personal perspective, a purposeful perspective, and a positional perspective. Your personal journey is really about your personal intentionality to experience the power of God in your life. Yes, God has plans for you, He has a destiny for you, and He has equipped you with spiritual gifts to aid you along this journey. However, it remains your responsibility to tap into all God has provided. As we conclude this journey of believing God, I would like to introduce you to George and Denice Bland.

George and Denice have been married for thirty-two years and have four children and four grandchildren. They are professing Christians who are active leaders in their local church, Bethlehem Star Baptist Church in Oklahoma City, where I currently pastor. On October 6, 2010, they received some devastating news. After a year of searching and going through several medical procedures, consulting with several doctors, and exercising personal persistence, Denice was diagnosed with leiomyosarcoma (LMS), a soft tissue cancer. As we move through the conclusion to this book, we will recall actual accounts of George and Denice's experience on their faith journey as it parallels each trimester of believing God.

Believing God from a personal perspective is all about a personal relationship with Jesus Christ. Unfortunately, many believers rely on the faith of someone else to bring them through whatever life challenge they may be facing at any given time. Many believers may have the same experience I had growing up. I had praying grandmothers. From my point of view, while I was living a contrary lifestyle, the Lord's grace was engulfing me because He was honoring the prayers of my grandmothers. I was not in an active personal relationship with Christ that afforded me the necessary access to call upon the Lord for myself. It's not that I didn't know I needed the Lord in my life--I just chose to live according to my own desires. While I was living my life, my grandmothers were praying for me.

Now don't get me wrong. I do believe my grandmothers' prayers worked on my behalf, but the prayers of others cannot substitute for a personal relationship with Christ. As a result of the prayers of others, many mistakenly credit their loved ones as the source of Christ. Believers often identify with individuals as their faith access point to Christ instead of recognizing the fact that a personal relationship with Christ is the only access point to Christ. The head knowledge of Christ is not enough to have a relationship with Christ. There must be a personal relationship with Christ established in the heart.

When George and Denice were faced with this LMS diagnosis, their faith was immediately tested. They were confronted with the reality of a diagnosis that would challenge the authenticity of their faith. During an interview with George and Denice, I asked them to "rate" their faith on October 6, 2010. Denice rated her faith level at a 3 or 4 on a 10-point rating system, while George rated himself a 7. I asked them to attempt to quantify their faith to help us establish a base line for their faith journey. At the time of their diagnosis I was preaching the series that has become this book, *90 Days of Believing God*. I started preaching the series on Sunday, August 29, 2010. As a part of the series, I added daily Scripture readings and one hour of personal prayer time before Wednesday night's prayer meeting and Bible study services. By the time of the diagnosis, we were already six weeks into this process. George and Denice were fully engaged and participated in this process. Please keep in mind that they were engaged prior to the diagnosis. Genuine faith is usually already active at the time of a crisis. Crisis faith becomes active once the crisis arrives.

George and Denice had a head start on the faith process through their already-established personal relationships with Christ. Although their personal relationships were intact, there were still different levels of active faith. Remember: George and Denice had been battling Denice's health issues for a year prior to the LMS diagnosis. Denice had already endured many medical procedures from biopsies to major invasive surgery, but all to no real avail. Although George and Denice don't claim all the process to this point was in vain, they still had not gotten to the root cause of her health issues. As a matter of fact, during this process prior to diagnosis George and Denice made the decision to change doctors because they knew something just wasn't adding up. At the point of diagnosis there were various procedures that, had they been done any differently, could have ended up spreading a cancer before Denice even knew she had cancer.

However, in their personal relationship with God, George and Denice were able to actively discern His voice. They recall making the decision to change doctors since they knew something was wrong. Ironically, during this whole time George was not worried. On the other hand Denice, a self-diagnosed worrier, admits she was frustrated and worried at times. Even in the midst of frustration and worry, she still had confidence that whatever was going on God was going to bring her through. Believing God from a personal perspective will afford believers the opportunity to hear the voice of God clearly. When they are actively engaged in a personal relationship with Christ, He is always leading them to a place of victory. Visibility to the full process was not given to George and Denice; they were willing to fully obey the instructions the Lord had already given.

Many times God's children will not understand what they are going through or why, but they must trust the process. Though circumstances may be difficult and understanding would seem to make things more bearable, they must trust that God has a plan and that it will work for their good and bring them to an expected end (Jerimiah 29:11). Obedience is key to the process of believing God. When the believer's relationship with Christ is solid, he or she will obey even when it seems impossible to understand. George and Denice would not know for some time how their journey would impact others--they were simply believing God.

As the journey of believing God continues, Christians must believe Him from a purposeful perspective, understanding that they themselves are not the central characters of their own journeys. Christ is the central character. Therefore, every part of this journey of believing God must have Christ as its primary focus. This misconception that the believer's victory is more about the believer than Christ is simply a misstated theory. It is Christ who gives the believer the opportunity to experience the power of God in what otherwise would be a life of damnation and condemnation. The believer must understand that believing God successfully is all about God being glorified. He allows the believer to experience Him in a personal way, so God himself can be glorified and others come to know Him. He makes this access available through His Son, Jesus Christ.

When God blesses the believer, He magnifies himself. It is critical for the believer on his or her journey of believing God not to get infected with the "I'm better than you" spirit. Many are deceived into believing that they are blessed because of their faithfulness or deservedness. All blessings of God are grace-based. Believing God requires the believer to understand that God has a purpose behind every blessing. God alone decided to deliver himself to others through others. The mature believer knows that God has a plan that is bigger than his or her situation. Yes, believers are the beneficiaries of the blessings of God and even have role to play in the blessing process, but the believer's role in no way supersedes the purpose of God. Ultimately, God's desire is to share himself with His body! Simply stated, God blesses believers to be a blessing to others that His name might be glorified!

When interviewing George and Denice, I asked a question regarding their thoughts of the diagnosis. Denice had an interesting perspective. On the front side of the journey Denice would ask the question "Why me, Lord?" As the process progressed, Denice's question evolved into yet another question: "Why *not* me, Lord?" When asked about the transition of her mind-set, she said there must be a reason for her going through this and that she was okay with it.

It is at this point many believers will stumble. When faced with adversity or unpleasant circumstances, it is somewhat natural for believers to question God as to why He would allow something of this magnitude to happen to them. Believers are typically so set in this too-blessed-to-be-adversely-impacted mind-set; they can't reconcile the fact that they too will suffer. Now the goal here is not to advocate for suffering. Though believers must understand that they are not exempt from suffering just because they believe, in their suffering believers must know that God has a purpose and a plan and that He will bring them through whatever He leads them to.

God will often use what appears to be negative situations just to demonstrate His mighty power. He will bring His children through trials and tribulations so others who may not know Him are given the opportunity to witness the power of God. He will also use similar situations to help believers who have never experienced Him on that level to move their faith needle to the next level. Every blessing of God must be shared with others. God's purpose will always be to give others access to His great salvation and all the benefits that accompany it. Many times believers are challenged to share their challenging life circumstances with others for many reasons. At some point they should share how God has blessed them.

Believers must believe with purpose. When the purpose of the blessing is more important than the actual blessing, the only way for others to get insight into how God operates is the believer's willingness to share his or her experiences. Failure to share blessings can delay the entire blessing process. When believers fail to give God the credit for the blessing, the blessing may be delayed in its arrival. Beyond the delay in receiving the blessing there could also be a delay in the blessing delivery. Having already established the fact that believers are blessed to bless others, failure to share could impact the delivery of blessings to those waiting on him or her to share. This failure could be considered disobedience. God uses the shared blessing as the seed to the believer's next blessing. The shared blessing starts the process of return. Luke 6:38 says, "Give, and it shall be given unto you; good measure, pressed down, and shaken together, and running over, shall men give into your bosom. For with the same measure that ye mete withal it shall be measured to you again." So while the sharing could be in testimony or intangible giving, both result in God's continuing the blessing circle. Testimonies give God all the credit, while tangible sharing gives others a tangible God experience. Share every blessing the Lord provides while giving God all the credit for all He has done, and the blessings will continue.

Finally, believers must believe God from a positional perspective. This addresses the position from which the believer believes. George and Denice's story took a major turn once they received the diagnosis. They were referred to the world-renowned MD Anderson Cancer Center in Houston. At a church service prior to their first trip to the center, I was attempting to encourage them by telling them that God was going to work this out and that everything was going to be okay. George politely corrected me as he boldly said, "They're not going to find anything, Pastor." Please keep in mind that George had no reason beyond his faith to make such a bold declaration. After all, George and Denice had just been referred to MD Anderson because their case required very specialized physicians and care. George was not believing God from a position of sickness and disease, but rather he was believing God from a position of healing.

What I really find interesting about George and Denice is how they both believed God but from different positions. While George humbly confesses that he believed God for complete healing from the onset, Denice says she knew without a doubt that God was going to heal her--but she believed she would have to endure a pretty difficult journey before the healing would be manifested.

As we look further into their journey, it was now December 2010 and time for the first MD Anderson trip, a long seven- to eight-hour drive from Oklahoma City. Once arriving in Houston, they spent several days of testing and on the last day had a face-to-face meeting with the doctor to discuss the results.

On this first trip the doctors came to George and Denice and informed them they were unable to locate the cancer! According to George's faith statement, the specialists were unable to find a cancer that was documented to be there. This process of taking the long drive, checking into the hotel, going to MD Anderson for testing, and seeing the doctor the last day has been going on for seven years at the time of this writing, with the same results each time--the inability to locate cancer! Initially this was a quarterly process and over time has been reduced to an annual process--but this trip to date has never yielded a positive cancer test!

It took eighteen months for the doctors to fully admit that they were simply unable to find the cancer. It was actually five years before the doctors could declare Denice cancer free! The irony in the whole testimony is that Denice has been going to MD Anderson over seven years for cancer treatment--but has never received any actual treatment or surgery for the cancer that once occupied her body. The cancer is well documented but at some point became undetectable.

God placed George and Denice on a path that has allowed them to help others who would believe God for their own miracle. Denice often answers others by saying, "Yes, I am a walking miracle." When believers choose to believe God from a position of God leading and them following, He will lead them in a way that blesses them personally, blesses the body of Christ, and ultimately allows others to experience the power of God!

Ultimately God will lead believers to a place to experience His glory. Be careful always to believe God from the correct position. God's plan includes His children believing Him from a position of following Him and not summoning Him. God desires to order the steps of believers, not respond to their every beck and call. Too many times they want to take shortcuts and not trust the process. God also desires for his children to believe Him from a delivered position and not a position of captivity. Believers can't approach God from the painful place of situational captivity. The enemy focuses on convincing Christians that their present conditions are somehow restricting their access to God. Jesus has already paid the price to afford deliverance over captivity. Additionally God desires His children to believe Him from a position of victory and not defeat! Believers should not pray as if they are losing, but rather they should believe God from a place of knowing they have already won the victory. The believer's victory is based not on individual efforts but rather the commitment of Christ to defeat the enemy once and for all!

Finally, Christians should believe God so they can see the glory of God. Every victory in Christ, every answered prayer, every redirect of a negative situation brings a manifestation of the glory of God on the scene. The challenge to every believer is to make his or her Christ relationship personal. Each believer will have a personal experience that does not look like anyone else's relationship. The beauty of God is that His resources and availability to His children are exhaustible. God is the God of more than enough, so He will never run short of anything the believer needs.

Believers must also remember that God is His own cause. Everything believers believe God for has the sole purpose of bringing God glory. Their experience should be exposed for others to see the glory of the Lord and not their own accomplishments. Finally, believers should let God take the lead, knowing He will always lead them to His best! God's desire is for His children to live in their destiny, impacting the world with their tailor-made God experience!

George and Denice serve as wonderful examples of this process. When I asked them to rate their faith after going through this process of healing, George's faith had gone from a 7 to a 10. Denice's faith had moved from a 3 or 4 to a 9 or 10. They said that although they believed God the whole time, there were still a few times when doubt tried to step in and rob them of faith along this journey. They let me know that though there were certainly some difficult days, God saw them through. When they look back over the entire process, they can see the hand of God so clearly. Some answers they didn't receive until after they had already experienced the victory. God was leading and they were following, but they really had no idea of what God was really doing.

In one instance Denice had a major invasive surgery. There were two possible approaches to the surgery: a traditional, more "old-fashioned" approach and a cutting-edge, more "modern" approach that had become the new "norm" for this particular procedure. The doctor elected to do the traditional form of the surgery.

Unbeknownst to George and Denise, had the surgeon elected to take the more modern approach to the procedure, it would have likely resulted in an immediate spread of the cancer that in many cases had already proven to be fatal. George and Denice didn't have access to this information at the time, but when God is leading, He has a way of navigating what believers cannot see.

On this journey of believing God it will be necessary for believers to fortify their personal relationship with Christ as they believe God from a personal perspective. Remember: God should always serve as the purpose for believing, and believers must see themselves where God says they are and not from where their circumstances place them.

Your journey of believing God is in your hands. Trust God, trust the process, and share the glory!

ABOUT the AUTHOR

Rev. Rodney R. Payne has a love for God, the people of God, and the work of God. His personal approach to ministry is focused on loving the people of God and equipping them for the work of the ministry.

Prior to yielding to God's call to preach, he served as an ordained deacon at The Loving St. James Baptist Church in Spencer, Oklahoma, for two years. Rev. Payne then accepted his call to the ministry and preached his first sermon November 27, 1996. He became an ordained minister July 28, 2002, at The Loving St. James Baptist Church under the pastorate of Rev. W. B. Parker.

Pastor Payne serves in many capacities in the work of the Lord. In 1999 he and Sister Thelma Payne founded One Voice Ministries, a non-profit marital and family enrichment ministry. His weekly Periscope broadcast, "Speaking with One

Voice," has a substantial following, enriching the lives of viewers. He also has established a leadership company, One Voice Leadership, in which he trains and equips leaders and organizations to achieve optimal performance within their companies.

His focus to prepare others for the kingdom of God is evidenced by his personal mission to equip individuals to experience the power of God, every day, in every area of their life.

Prior to becoming a full-time pastor, Rev. Payne served in outreach and street ministries and as a Sunday School teacher, youth pastor, and associate minister. He also served as assistant pastor at Bethlehem Star Baptist Church for three years prior to being called to pastor the church in December 2008. He was officially installed as pastor January 11, 2009.

Since becoming pastor, the church campus has grown with the expansion of the existing facility with the addition of areas for youth and children's ministries as well as a new administrative area. With the acquisition of three adjacent parcels of land, Bethlehem Star is positioned to grow yet again to support even more of the community's needs.

Pastor Payne established a new program, Operation Increasing the Body of Christ, a successful outreach program that has led to a tremendous growth in membership. In 2014 his vision to continuously reach the populace of the metro area led to the three-day event Praise Beyond the Walls, partnering with local and private businesses, law enforcement agencies, and churches in an effort to provide support in the communities. This free epic outreach event focused on meeting the needs of the community by ministering to the whole person. The vision for Praise Beyond the Walls was expanded to a weeklong event that included everything from health and wellness checks to professional development, a job fair, entrepreneur development, a leadership conference, and much more. Pastor Payne also hosted another community-focused initiative "It Will Get Better" (in collaboration with metro-area law enforcement personnel) that confirmed and showed support to local police officers as well as showing communities that they are not alone and that the law officials are there to serve and protect them.

Pastor Payne currently serves as Regional Director for the National Evangelism Movement, Incorporated.

He is the husband of Sister Thelma Payne. They have been married for twenty-seven years and have two beautiful daughters and one son-in-law, Danielle (Trevel) and Devin.

Twitter@PastorRPayne
Periscope@PastorRPayne
Instagram@PastorRodneyPayne
Facebook.com/PastorRodneyPayne